My way
to the
SEVEN SEAS

A Brazilian Boy's Tale of
Resilience, Achievement & Adventure

Martinês Rocha de Souza

Like to know more about
My Way to the Seven Seas?
This 3 minute video is a taster
for Martinês' story.

RenBro
PUBLISHING

Front cover: Geiranger, Norway (Dalsnibba Mountain)
Back cover from top to bottom: Cairo, Egypt; Petra, Jordan; Amazon, Brazil;
Geiranger fjords, Norway

Martinês Rocha de Souza

MY WAY TO THE SEVEN SEAS
A Brazilian Boy's Tale of Resilience, Achievement and Adventure

Originally Published in Portuguese in May 2013
in Brazil as "O Caminho Para os Sete Mares"

First Published in English in December 2013

New and Fully Revised Edition in English 2015
Published by RenBro Publishing
www.renbro.com.au
info@renbro.com.au

Interior and online photography: Martinês Rocha de Souza
Online videos: Martinês Rocha de Souza
Facebook Page: MY WAY TO THE SEVEN SEAS
YouTube Page: Martines Rocha
Email: martinesrocha@gmail.com
Web: www.martinesrocha.com.br

This is a non-fictional story told by the author.
All of the characters, organizations and events
portrayed in this book are real and the story is factual.

ISBN: 978-1-925198-00-3

My way to the SEVEN SEAS

My Way to the Seven Seas
micro-site and photo gallery:
www.renbro.com.au/sevenseas

DEDICATION

When life puts difficulties in our way, help comes in many forms—including challenges, because an easy path can make us lazy and unable to evolve. That is why I thank God for the difficulties put in my way.

My family gave me the support I needed to reach the place where I am standing now, even though they did not have many resources. I was educated to face life with dignity and hard work, without cheating or taking possession of what was not mine. My family taught me how to be happy with what I do and who I am.

For all these reasons, I dedicate these memories of mine:

To my Mum, Mrs Nilde, the warrior who, in the silence of her pains, sacrificed her life to let me live my life. My Mum is still alive, just to let you know. It may seem from this dedication that perhaps she isn't!

To the memory of my Uncle Didi, whose legacy lives on in the values that nourished our family.

Having fun with Mum in Salvador

Uncle Didi and Auntie Aldir

MY THANKS

To my brother Denilton Rocha. With eternal gratitude, he has become a shining ever bright example to me: father, brother, friend, all at the same time. His values of honesty and respect have given me a base for life and living and has made it possible for me to venture far beyond geographical boundaries.

To my sister Bila whose encouraging words through hard times have made me stronger.

To my friend, the designer Erone Feitosa, without whose support this book would never have been written.

To my childhood friend, the writer Emerson Fernando, who helped me to start this project, spending many afternoons sitting at his mother's coffee table. As he says, quoting John Donne: "no man is an island".

To the writer Joaquim Maria Botelho, who made poetry out of my modest words.

To David Bennett whose passion for my writing helped me to first edit my book into English.

To RenBro Publishing for believing in this book and, through this new and fully revised edition, turning my book into a unique and very special reading experience.

Finally, to all my friends past and present.

My sincere thanks to you all.

HOW TO USE THIS BOOK

This is a new generation book—a multimedia experience. A book where you can read the words on the page, like every other book. But if you'd like to immerse yourself in the Author's world, you can look at his stunning photographs from around the world. You can also view videos, filmed by the Author himself, which will convey an even richer experience than the words on the page.

You may already be familiar with QR codes, the knobbly little boxes that appear all over the place: marketing brochures, advertising billboards, corporate PR materials, and even on the sides of public buses. If so, no instructions are needed. But for many of you, this may be your first experience with these useful little tools.

A QR (Quick Response) code is a block of usually black and white squares. This code stores information that can be retrieved by the many free QR reader apps[1] available for your smart-phone or tablet. By scanning the code, the QR reader will deliver the information to you: photos, videos, web pages and more. For example, you may have discovered that the QR code on the front cover of this book will show you a short dynamic video of what you can expect in the book.

So, you are invited to take the plunge with this new way of 'reading' a book, using your smart-phone or tablet. Or you can enter the accompanying web address onto your computer and watch the videos on a bigger screen with better sound. Enjoy this exciting new way of reading a book!

Black-headed codes will take you to a video

Sample video code

vimeo.com/113986161

Grey-headed codes will take you to a photo

Sample photo code

bit.ly/1zeYfTe

---

[1] Note that the QR codes in this book have been thoroughly tested. However not all QR readers/scanners are of equal quality. If you find that your scanner has persistent difficulty loading photos or videos, please try another app.

CONTENTS

PREFACE

THE WORLD BELONGS TO THE ADVENTURERS

Since the time of the Phoenicians, masters of navigation have explored the seas. Amongst them the Vikings, the Greeks, and later the Portuguese, launched their vessels into waters inhabited by monsters. They challenged the belief that the world was flat and ended in a huge waterfall where all ships that dared to sail would fall and disappear to face the gods.

In our contemporary world, my leading character of maritime adventure is Amyr Klink. I had the honor to interview him in my time as a reporter for the Brazilian news-magazine Manchete. This was on his arrival in Salvador, Bahia, after his famous crossing of the Atlantic Ocean, a journey of one hundred days rowing from Dakar, Senegal. Amyr had survived the challenges of the sea.

Martinês Rocha de Souza has not done this, but like Amyr, and in consideration of the challenges of perceived limitations, Martinês and Amyr are quite the same.

I cannot say that Martinês is a hero in the classic sense of the word. He has not fought in, nor lead armies to war, he has not brought about a political regime. However, he has in a way lived his own life with intensity. What makes him a man of courage is his ability to simply resist the desire to give up in moments of oppression, prejudice and contempt, and when the disbelief of others comes near to him. He is a man who has overcome adversity, and with the Christian ethic of forgiveness and turning the other cheek, he has not resorted to vengeance, which has been an option, as it is to all.

I met Martinês almost by chance. He contacted the Brazilian Writers Association, where I work, hoping to find a writer willing to help him with his book, to correct the text and tell him how to organize the narrative. I became interested in helping him myself when I met him, because I saw in front of me a young man filled with enthusiasm, with a story already written, but lacking experience with the use of language in book form. He needed assistance in organizing his ideas and presenting them coherently into a text for publication.

We started working together and I edited various points in his book, but never interfered in it. The way the story is told is the choice of the author, and what you will read is his way of seeing the world. Before contacting me he had asked for help from some friends, however he come to realize, and this is a fine quality he has, that his manuscript needed impartial and dispassionate attention. The result is before you. Of course, the story has not yet ended. It is open, as open as his young heart is towards the world.

Who is this guy, anyway?

He is an ordinary man.

He was born in a small inland village, in Bahia state, Brazil. Like most children there, he dreamed about becoming a professional soccer player, so he could earn piles of money and date lots of beautiful girls. But he said to me, somebody out there, or up there, had some different plans for him.

At the age of 21, he was just like other northeast Brazilian fellows, a migrating bird looking for a spot under the sun, and southbound he went. He moved to São Paulo central. Feeling alone and afraid, and in the middle of an ocean of people he found some who also carried in their hearts that same dream of his: money and fame.

In São Paulo, he found no soccer. No money. No fame. No gorgeous women. Instead, hunger, poverty, shame and a seemingly fruitless search. But, stubborn as a mule, he finally found a job as a car-parking attendant and he started to study English and got himself another job, as the bellboy of an international hotel. He made contacts, attended school, and did what he has come to do so well: learn.

A few years later, he made his first trip on an ocean liner, as a member of the crew, working as a bar waiter. And he has never looked back.

Since 2009, he has taken courses to develop his skills as a bartender, a fire warden and in sea rescue. During his travels, he has been able to visit some 300 cities in 80 countries on six continents. He has taken more than 40,000 pictures and produced about five thousand videos, many of them exhibited in his YouTube page: Martines Rocha.

You are about to read the story of a common guy, with good qualities, but with faults and vices. At the same time though, he is a person equipped with an invincible determination to succeed and also be happy. He found paths because he found the right people and he found the right people while he was finding his path. Where there were roads, he asked how to find them. Where there were no roads, he learnt how to build them.

This is the story of a strong man. Likely we could all learn something from his adventures.

Joaquim Maria Botelho
Brazilian journalist and writer
São Paulo

PUBLISHER'S NOTE

This is Martinês' story, told in his own words. As English is his second language, some departures from grammatical conventions have been permitted. This allows Martinês' genuine and unique voice to be heard as you the reader come to know him.

INTRODUCTION

A glimpse to the future, without forgetting the past

I introduce my story by setting the scene.

Time: present day.

Environment: Queen Mary 2, the greatest ocean liner ever built in the world, and currently docked in Southampton in England.

My space reference: my cabin 533, Deck A, on-board Queen Mary 2.

What am I doing: starting to adapt my book, "My Way to the Seven Seas", for the English language.

My immediate expectation: waiting for my friends to finish their working day and join me to celebrate my birthday in the crew bar.

My resolution: to complete my book for its first publication in English by December 2013.

It may seem the most trivial thing in the world, a guy like me sitting at his desk, in his cabin on a ship, waiting to start writing the introduction for an English version of his book; a book that had already been published in Portuguese earlier in that same year. Not a usual situation, right? Of course that is right!

I have to begin my story.

When I was a boy I grew up in a very small inland village called Boninal in the State of Bahia in Brazil. In spite of my origin, I could say modest beginnings, I managed to break through many social and economic barriers by means of discipline, hard work, determination and seriousness. To me, I believe that I have now reached a previously unimaginable social position.

I hope some of you, if not all, through the following pages, will find what I tell you and the way I have accomplished my achievements, a motivating factor to encourage you to escape the claws of fate and sail your own oceans of accomplishment.

But now, allow me to make a brief personal presentation.

I am 34 years old and I have no children—that I know of, at least. But why do I bring to this book the subject of paternity? My explanation is in two parts and quite simple.

Firstly, the date on which I wrote this introduction, August 8th 2013, is special. It is the anniversary of my own birthday.

Secondly, I have been talking to my friend Benedict from the Philippines, about children. When he heard that I was approaching 34 years, he asked me if I had children. I said no. He was quite sincere in saying, at my age I should be considering getting married and having kids. His recommendation is in support of a tradition throughout Brazil, as in the rest of the world. It reminds one that having a family is perhaps the obligation of every adult person. In my case, I have delayed this. I should be married by now, as all my friends are. Benedict is 32 years old and in spite of being younger than me, he already has an eight year-old boy. He assured me that I, even without a wife, should provide a kid to the world. I replied that life as we know back home is not the same when you work on a ship. Life on-board is well removed from what we had known to be normal.

My life is made very busy with other priorities. I lived in my village to the age of 21. I had never thought about children and resisted my friends' pressure to form a family as they did. Of course I wanted children, but in the future. This may have been the legacy of my father, who abandoned my mother when I was three years old. I will be back to this subject, later in the book. What I consider to be a lesson from my father is that I decided it would be easier for me to carry responsibilities by myself, without involving anyone else and not risking hurting others. And when the time is right I hope the right person will come to me. Then perhaps I will marry.

When I turned 21, I decided to work in São Paulo. After a two-day journey, I arrived at the central bus terminal. It was like seeing the world for the first time. The city is huge, with more than 13 million people in the metropolitan area. The bus terminal was crowded as I had never seen before. But I had to cope with everything, especially my own fears.

When I arrived in São Paulo, one of my first concerns was the fact that I had not yet completed high school. Because of that, I knew for certain that my life was not going to be easy in the big city. Probably, I would have to resign myself to being a shelf stacker. I was not completely useless though, because I knew how to drive and already had a license, but I was extremely afraid of facing the big city traffic. Who would be mad enough to give a truck to me to drive? There were so many questions, and barriers, created by my own fear that I felt really stressed all the time.

This early pessimism isn't really part of who I am. It serves only to make my current moment clear. The truth for me is the other way around: I am an optimist and I see life with my eyes focused on the future, to the light that shines like a sun on the horizon. I do know, however, that much of what we plan and hope for, may never be accomplished. I was never a shelf stacker, but I worked instead as a waiter, bellboy, a driver and a parking attendant. All stepping-stones to my goal of the life I wanted.

I overcame these first moments of sadness and managed to get hired in a car parking business. I drove small distances, terrified of scratching one of those big cars that I used to see only on TV. Something, however, was missing. In a big city like São Paulo, one soon discovers that it is necessary to develop. So I had to seek training and education.

Currently, I am a technician in hospitality. I help to run, as a partner, a small hotel in São Paulo metropolitan area (www.hotelimperialinn.com.br). I am also a bartender graduated from two schools in Brazil. And, at this very moment, I am nothing but a guy preparing himself to celebrate his birthday at the crew bar, on-board the Cunard liner Queen Mary 2. I have been on duty on this vessel since July 13th, 2013. Cunard has been my employer since 2010, when I started working on the liner Queen Victoria.

In my time as a parking attendant, I went back to school. My decision to study was driven by my urgency to switch jobs and make money. It was at that point that I made contact with the English language. I took some courses that made me grow up, not only professionally, but personally too. It was something that I have never imagined. I did not have intimacy with my own native language and was already speaking like the "gringos". Fate has its ironies. Nowadays I have a true devotion to the English language. I learn something new everyday.

What I intend to do with this book is to tell my story and experiences with passengers and crew members, showing that even a poor person like myself can achieve success. Or better: poor people are just as entitled to happiness as anyone else.

I will go on working and, who knows, I will be able to help people like me who come from poverty. Many people who work on liners have a history similar to mine. Maybe they can take advantage of something in my life to inspire their lives. I do not have the pretension of thought that I will be changing anybody's life. Each person is the architect of his or her own destiny. Success is not for those who follow my steps, but rather for those who recognize their own internal strength. In my case, I have identified that strength, and directed it. As the reader might see in this book, any person with dedication and discipline can go further and further, perhaps more than the 300 countries of the globe, without being a millionaire. It requires work and imagination.

Today, in spite of the passion I have for life and for people, I consider myself a man each day colder. Cold in the sense that nothing impresses me anymore. I have learned to control my emotions. After being in Egypt five times, after visiting Rome, the Vatican, London, Oslo, Los Angeles, after serving the most distinguished passengers throughout the world, now I can say: nothing impresses me much anymore as they did in my earlier days.

Today I face the world with much more naturalness and even consider possible some things that appeared before to be intangible. As a friend of mine says, "Martin, you are now so cosmopolitan". What she is talking about is that she saw me trembling, frightened, hesitant, on my first day as an English language student, at the Brazilian School of Commerce—Senac.

I am now more sure of myself. I speak good English and a bit of Spanish, enough to keep out of trouble in Hispanic countries. I can say that so far I have accomplished many of my projects. There is still a lot more to do. Projects are fuel for me. Of course, I still have a long way to go to complete all my dreams. Maybe by the time I die I may have only completed 10 per cent of my dreams. But, when the Man "up there" calls me, I will have a clear conscience that I tried everything I could to reach what is worthwhile.

My projects get bigger and bigger because as I conclude one, the next seems to be easier in comparison. My main project of the moment is this book that I deliver to the hands of my readers.

Very soon, I will be once again embarked, back to the seas, heading East, ready to visit Asia, on a world cruise that will start on January 10th and will continue till May 9th. After that, I still have part of Africa and Alaska to visit. I'm not trying to sound pompous, it is just that exotic places are no longer unreachable for me as they once were.

As for the future, and I mean for the near future, I plan to work on ships for two or three more contracts. This may alter, because something always changes on-board. (I will explain, in the next chapters, how life is for a seaman). With these contracts I will be able to afford my apartment, a place that I could call my own, a place to be my refuge, the same as my family house, in my home village of Boninal, in the warm state of Bahia. Those contracts will allow me also to know other places of the world, to live with people of more than fifty different nationalities that form the traveling microcosm that is a ship.

Studying opened doors that I didn't even know existed. Working in big hotels in Brazil and on ships throughout the world has given me the opportunity of experiencing amazing things. There is no greater learning. I am privileged because I have been to places that I read about only in history books. Such experiences make me believe in the existence of God. And yet I still feel like the boy from Boninal, who never expected to see so many wonders. Nevertheless, I have always had the traveling spirit. The unknown attracts me.

I have no talent for poetry, but I can see poems in every image that I capture around the world.

By the way, Boninal means "a field of daisies".

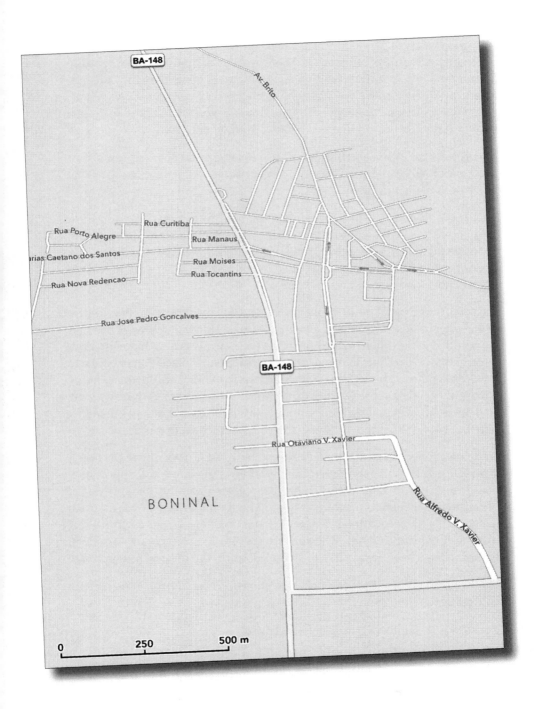

First Part:
Childhood

TRINIDAD

Caracas

VENEZUELA

Georgetown

Paramaribo
FRENCH GUIANA

Bogoto

SURINAME
Cayenne

COLOMBIA

GUYANA

Quito

ECUADOR

PERU

B R A Z I L

BAHIA

Lima

Boninal

La Paz

Brasilia

BOLIVIA

PARAGUAY

CHILE

Asuncion

ARGENTINA

Santiago

Buenos-Aires

URUGUAY

SOUTH AMERICA

FALKLAND Is.

First Communion in Boninal

bit.ly/1x2TaaT

Chapter 1

My childhood in Down Street, Boninal

"Marta, I am wasted here, in a town so small..."

That was what I said many times to my cousin Marta Cristina. She was my friend, my listener, and the one who understood my anxieties. She smiled, hearing me talk about my dreams of greatness. We were then only kids.

I was convinced that I could be more than just one of the 3,000 inhabitants of Boninal, handcuffed to an inescapable routine and to an unsalted and uninteresting destiny. I saw in me a kind of skill, a gift if you prefer, something that made me expect more from the world and from life. "My skills need space", I used to say to my cousin. She smiled, with the acquiescence of one who loved me.

My hometown is a lovely place, but it did not satisfy my expectations. São Paulo always was the aim for my future.

Of all my dreams, close and distant, the one I aspired to the most was winning in São Paulo. By the news that came to me, it was a rich and powerful place. In the year 2000, when I dared to move to São Paulo, the city had only 18 elders for each group of 100 children. This meant that less than 9% of the population was above 60 years of age. São Paulo was a land of young people.

The time I referred to in the beginning of this chapter was the mid 1990s. I was a kid looking for success in the big city. I searched all the information I could about it. I had a rough idea of the difficulties a migrant should face there. But it was just ideas. I could not know what would happen to a naive guy like me in the middle of a nervous, busy, crowded, greedy city.

For me, it was certain that, by the age of 18, I should have won my independence and should be able to do whatever I wished with my life. I was convinced that receiving my driver's license would be like receiving a social certificate of adulthood. It would be my enfranchisement letter freeing me from the monotony and pettiness of my hometown. With my driver's license, I felt like I was sitting on the magic carpet of ancient tales, flying the skies to the South.

Independence was my goal ... but how to reach it in my village?

There were some ties keeping me captive, like rusty anchors. The most important of them was my mother's resistance to let me go. She grabbed with both hands the imaginary wings of the little bird I was.

But there were also other moorings to break. Uncles and cousins who knew the south-eastern part of Brazil repeated to me: "São Paulo is a place where sons weep and mothers won't hear". Perhaps their intention was to give me more time, hoping that I would change my mind. They advised me to finish high school before thinking of leaving. Without the certificate, it was going to be very difficult to find a decent job in the South.

My journey to begin my life to independence was not without other difficulties. The way to São Paulo was complicated. I would have to take a bus and travel some 40 miles in an old dirt road, then take another bus for a 28-hour trip. Tickets were expensive. And there at the end of the highway, a city that I could not say was hostile, but I could not say was friendly to those who challenge it. São Paulo requires strength, determination and courage.

My friends, some of them driven by their needs, had already been there and knew that life is not easy for anyone. Professional success in the megalopolis is nearly impossible for a young man from the countryside. I knew little to nothing about life there and had almost no education—remember that I did not complete high school before leaving.

And finally, the main obstacle for my independence: my own brother.

The captain of the boat of my life

Before telling you about the shock that motivated me to "run away" from Boninal, I have to make it clear that I have never thought badly of my mother for not encouraging my departure to São Paulo. I know she loved me and that her only intention was to preserve my well-being, worried as she was about my happiness. I have to write a bit more about her because she is my reference point and biggest inspiration. Although illiterate, my mother devoted her life to kindle in me a desire for education. She came from a poor patriarchal family, and her first phase of life was no different from the majority of the women of her time. Women were expected to marry, bear children, and take care of the house, kids and husband. Those were the general rules, commandments taught as doctrines in such a way that became embodied in their personalities. My mother, therefore, behaved almost by instinct to follow her "obligations". She was not blessed with a regular standard family. I never knew the reasons why she and my father separated when I was three years old, and I never wanted to find out why. In relation to this, I seem to have no trauma or bad feelings whatsoever. What remains, crystallized in my soul, is a certain fear, mixed with a deep sense of responsibility, of starting a family.

I do not judge my father. One should not judge when all the information is not available. But I wish to emphasize my deepest admiration and respect for the one who never deserted me: my mother. I learned that a captain never abandons the ship. My mother was the captain, my captain, holding the rudder of my life, courageous, determined. She raised three children single-handed, almost without money and knowledge, and was able to teach us the most dignifying values providing us with ethics and morals.

I do not want to idealize my mother as a super-woman. But it is unarguable that she is a serious, firm and courageous person, standing true all the time. She did not bend in the face of life's difficulties—and those were many. I do not feel ashamed of using the old cliché: she is my heroine. Even though we have many relatives throughout the world, for me and for my brother, our mother's singularity resides in her attitudes of eternal welcome and shelter. My mother is my history, our history, our beginning, our middle and our end. She is our safe harbor, no matter where we are in the world.

Denilton, my half dad

My brother Denilton Rocha de Souza has been the man for our family since he was a boy. He is a strong guy, physically and mentally speaking. Intelligent, hard working, determined, he fights for what he believes. He had a fatherly outlook over my sister and me; me in particular because I was the youngest and rebellious. With that attitude, he was the masculine role model we needed; although he

Working with Denilton

himself did not have such a reference in his childhood and adolescence.

By circumstances of being in the position of elder brother, he felt responsible for the family and assumed his obligation to look after us. He was concerned about me slipping up and warned me of two things I should avoid: fights and drugs. He would not forgive me if I would get involved in either of those things. I swear I learnt this lesson.

By the way, he was the one who taught me everything that was really important when I was growing up. He taught me everything that I use for my own good. He is a man of sensitivity and a music lover. His musical idol is the Brazilian singer and composer Cazuza.

Denilton never made it easy for me. He made me begin work at a very early age. I remember that we worked together in a snack bar. My sister baked cakes and I was in charge of delivering the cakes to the clients. My brother used to work in a snack bar, in a gas station in our home village, providing food and drinks to his clients. I used to be the one bringing the cakes to him by bike. Even though he could do it himself and there were other ways to provide the delivery, Denilton insisted on me doing it. I understand now his intention of occupying me with productive tasks and teaching me how to work.

After some time, my brother managed to save up some money and bought a partnership in a bakery shop. Our village needed people like him, full of enthusiasm and courage to invest and work. So together with someone else, he opened his first business in this bakery shop. He took me with him, and my duty was to weigh and wrap up the biscuits that we produced. I used to work in the mornings, my brother wanted to watch me closely. He did not want to let me take the wrong path into drugs or robbery or other no good ways. He always wanted to know where I was and what I was doing. With his enterprising spirit, very soon he then opened a candy shop. Because he continued to work in the bakery shop, he decided to put my sister and me in charge of the candy shop. Bila, my sister, took care of the shop in the mornings. I worked in the bakery shop in the mornings, took care of the candy shop in the afternoons and went to school at nights. The period I am talking about here is from 1994 to 1997. During these years I used to go to school at night. I did not like this in the first place because my schoolmates attended in the afternoon; anyway I got used to it. I remember my thoughts at that time: "Poor me! When will I ever be able to play?" Do not take pity on me, though, because I had plenty of time for my games and tricks.

I had my time for playing soccer at 5:00pm between candy shop and school that started at 6:50pm. After one hour for playing I took a quick shower and then ate before heading off to school. I did not work in the bakery on weekends though so I had more time to play then!

In parallel with all that, Denilton observed the town growing and decided to establish his first construction materials shop. At that time, only two shops existed in Boninal. It was 1998 and this business gave my brother and our family some financial security. By then, I knew how to drive and even though I did not have a driver's license, I was the one driving his trucks. This was cheaper for my brother and I loved it because I was driving big and nice vehicles. All this made me feel useful and important to our family. It was a strategic decision because this enterprise, the famous Casa Brasil (Brazil House), gave Denilton both good profits and experience. He decided to postpone his dream of leaving his hometown. All the members of our family worked at Casa Brasil. Bila was a salesperson and I took care of the deliveries with the help of Salvador, my dear friend, a tall and strong man, with a huge heart. By this time my brother had already left the partnership in the bakery shop. We all helped out in that business and it worked till 2009. My brother is opening another one soon in another place.

I admit that it was one of the best periods of my life. I got to know all the slums (favelas) around the town. I cannot express enough how much I have learned from my brother, regarding sales. He is pretty good at it. Today, when I am considered to be one of the best salespersons on the ship where I work, I understand how much I owe my brother for his lessons. I will write about this subject a little later but I assure you that, if I was to number everything I learned from him, I would have to write another book: driving, riding bicycles, swimming and, most important of all, fishing. I still hear him saying: 'Catch the fish, not only eat the fish'. In spite of all the difficulties, there were always fish in our meals. I knew very well where it came from and how hard it was to catch. Today, I realize that I am a fisherman who lives on the high seas. This means that I know the importance of work and living life as a good person with values of honesty and integrity—even when things are tough! My brother, my Mum and my Uncle taught me these things and I know that these have helped me realize my life dreams.

My brother had another fundamental supporter who helped him provide for the family: our Uncle Didi, the youngest brother of our mother. He is a most important person in our lives. When our father went away, he took the reins of the family as if it were his mission in life. He taught Denilton honesty and the uncountable value of work. He acted with the nobility of a great man who knew that "The more worthy are the hands that help than the lips that pray". He was our lighthouse in the way of goodness and right. A cheerful man, calm, patient and always smiling, he showed us, with his attitude, how to behave correctly. We have, towards him, a deep feeling of gratitude. Didi left us, lamentably, in February 2011. His time to leave this earth had come.

Evolving without changing my mind

Like every kid, I spent a good part of my life considering my brother a pain in the ass. I did not understand the reason for such strictness. Now I know he tried to be a good father-substitute, and he did not get to enjoy much leisure time; he abdicated his adolescence and part of his adult life to make sure that we could live well. Maybe the words I use here are not enough to sufficiently describe my gratitude and feelings towards this man. He sacrificed part of his life for us. Even if I were a great writer, perhaps I could not register in words how I am grateful to him. But…there is always a but in our lives!

The but is, Denilton wouldn't accept my decision to leave Boninal. He had given us a comfortable life—what else could I wish for? Going away, leaving behind everything he built for us, seemed to him like a betrayal.

I am very much like Denilton. I dare say that I am an improved version of him, because I had what he did not: time to learn other things and time to socialize while he was working and providing for us.

My brother is very rigid. To him, my leaving seemed disloyal given, after all, that he gave me everything. That is my conclusion, looking at the past with my eyes today, I finally understand his sorrow at my departure. In my defense, I mention that it was he who taught me to be brave, to be a fish swimming down the river in search of the ocean.

I really believed the words I used to say to my cousin Marta, that my hometown was too small for me. I needed somehow to go away. My dream of conquering São Paulo never faded.

From Saint John's day to Christmas Eve

Three years later in 2000 I was in the penultimate year of high school. It was June, and the most important party of the north-eastern Brazilian region happens on the 24th, a day dedicated to Saint John. That night, I went to a bar that was the meeting place for us youngsters and I met up with a fellow called Fábio, who already lived in São Paulo. I confessed my true desire to do the same. Very diplomatically, he described the negative and positive aspects. I heard his words with my heart. That talk with Fábio was decisive for me.

I thought of a sailor who I admire very much, Amyr Klink. He wrote, in one of his books, "One day we need to stop dreaming and leave".

I still don't know exactly why I decided to go. The fact is that a few days before Christmas I quit school, bought a ticket and told Marta that I was going to São Paulo. She gave me a book of prayers that she wrote herself, a souvenir that I still carry with me all the time. In the gray dawn of December 21 in the year 2000 I walked alone to the bus station. The town was immersed in a dark atmosphere. My mother said goodbye at home—she did not want to see me off at the bus station.

Marta, my cousin is now married, and is a mother to Pedro. She works as a primary school teacher in our hometown.

Martinês and Marta at the launch of the Portuguese edition of *My Way to the Seven Seas*

Chapter 2

Destination São Paulo

The bus station, only three blocks away from my house, was a point of departure and also a point of sadness. I was suffering but I had made my choice. I was going to follow my dream at all costs.

I arrived with just a backpack filled with clothes. In my hand I also had a present from my mother: a small container with farofa, a side dish made of manioc flour, typical home food. In my pocket I had 150 dollars that my brother gave me. He played tough though and did not say goodbye. Even so, in the end he had supported my decision.

My mind was busy with millions of thoughts. This didn't prevent me from remembering a phrase of one of my brother's friends: "You won't stay longer than two days in São Paulo".

I do not lie when I say that that sentence was motivational. I confess to being scared at that moment. But in the end it worked as a lever to push me, a big trampoline throwing me forward. It may have been the challenge I needed to hear.

There was something else cooking my brains though. Where would I work, without a high school certificate, counting only on a provisional driver's license? At least Fábio had arranged a place for me to stay. He was going to meet me in São Paulo, the land of mist. I stepped onto the bus. Not accustomed to travel, it took me some time to locate my seat. A few minutes later, the bus left the bus station, perhaps one of the smallest in the whole world. My journey began.

In the first stretch of the journey, jiggling on the dirt road, I thought about what I had done and what I was doing. I was apprehensive. I longed for this trip and I chose to make it, but the way I left Boninal made me sad. After some hours of anguish, I was distracted with the landscape that often changed. Many places I had only heard of were now passing me by. I started to cheer up. Sadness fades away when life shows novelties to us.

That first nightfall, the bus crossed the borderline with another state, Minas Gerais. I felt almost an epiphany. I was tired, and usually I sleep very easily, but I could not fall asleep that night. The dawn was up when I finally shut my eyes. When I woke the bus was already in the state of Rio de Janeiro, in an industrial city called Volta Redonda. Again anxiety took over as less than ten hours separated me from São Paulo. I could not go back to sleep. From that point on, I enjoyed the landscape, so different from what I used to see in my home state of Bahia. I was especially moved by the Presidente Dutra Highway, a marvelous road that I had seen many times on TV.

The bus made a final stop in Aparecida. This is the place where the image of Our Lady Aparecida, patron saint of Brazil, was found in a river in 1717, nearly 300 years ago. I bought a meal, extremely expensive for my modest budget. The proximity of São Paulo made me tremble. Three hours later, we arrived.

Land of mist was what I was expecting. Wrong! The sky was clear and the weather very warm. I got off the bus. The terminal was incredibly crowded. Thousands of people were coming from or going to places to spend the holidays. The day was a Friday, December 22, almost Christmas! Walking, I bumped into people rushing to embark, and what comes to me is the image of a ship…

Nobody was waiting for me at the platform. I looked at the crowd, not a single known face did I see. So I waited. Nobody came. I waited some more, already tense. Nobody to call for safe harbor. By then I was in a panic.

All of a sudden, I noticed a man watching me with an inquisitive air. Who could he be? An opportunist, maybe a thief? Many people warned me about the risks of robbery at the São Paulo bus terminal. Finally, after a little while, the man came closer to me and asked, a little shyly, if my name was Martini. I said yes, knowing that he confused my name with the name of an alcoholic drink! He smiled and identified himself as Jailton, Fábio's uncle. I remembered seeing him in Boninal once, but I was a child then and I hadn't remembered what he looked like. At least he knew the number of my bus, and it was easy for him to disregard people who didn't fit my description. My relief was huge as I hugged him very tightly. He explained that Fábio had been asked to work late that day at the pet shop, and could not come to meet me. Fábio himself was not able to tell me about this, because very few people could afford to have a mobile phone in those days.

Jailton showed me the way to the subway. It was fine and fast stuff! I loved the nice clean train, a far cry from our trains at home.

□ □ □ ☐ □ □ □

Destination Sao Paulo

vimeo.com/114737401

My brother
Denilton

My sister
"Bila"

My mother
Mrs Nilde

Xmas 2012

Chapter 3

Sad Christmas

I have to write about my sister. She does not like her name of Maria José. She prefers her nickname Bila, derived from the lyrics of a Brazilian popular song.

Always by my side, she was the voice that guided my steps towards self-improvement, but also helped me to understand the feminine soul in my love adventures. I will never forget a kind of "how-to-seduce-a-girl handbook" that she wrote for me. Do not think me big-headed but I guess I learned very well the content of the lessons. Even so do not take me for a Don Juan, but the truth is that I feel that I really have had success with the opposite sex.

Of course, we had our differences. Bila is one year older than me. But even so just a look between us would sometimes be enough for us to understand each other. And today I comprehend how valuable and truthful her advice was to me, even when she gave it harshly. I would also like to thank her, in writing, for her patience when trying to help me with my school homework, although she knew that it was a pointless task, because I had no desire to study back then. Today, however, the bad disciple has the pleasure of teaching the master on some points.

Below, is a letter that Bila sent me, telling me what my departure represented for our family in Boninal.

Christmas Eve was coming, and with it came the emptiness left by the departure of my youngest brother from our home. Such a thing had never happened before to us. We were always a very close family and none of us has been apart for more than a week. Christmas was never a cheerful day for us. But that year 2000 was especially marked by sadness, because of Martinês' absence. The family felt fragmented for quite a while.

Martinês was the source of enlightenment in our house. His merry attitude was full of life and he made any place festive.

I know that with him leaving us our hearts broke and we felt helpless. But he had his reasons to go away. Working for the family meant guaranteeing food. Martinês wanted more than that. He was already an adult, full of ambitions, like his friends in São Paulo and dreaming about that Promised Land. I remember that our oldest brother took Martinês decision as a kind of betrayal. They stood apart for some time, spoiling the beautiful friendship they had.

I confess that I was against Martinês decision at first. I admit that more than once I imposed my points of view on him, as an older sister sometimes does in a most radical way. Which shook our friendship too. Today I thank God it is all over.

My brother decided to leave our hometown because of the lack of resources and opportunities. Boninal is a shy town and does not offer many professional opportunities.

Martinês is a resolute man. When he decides to do something he sees it through. Never leaving till tomorrow what he can do today, he always fought to reach the goal he planned for. If he says "I go", one can be sure he goes indeed.

Second Part:
Sao Paulo

Chapter 4

Nobody can stand alone

Where was I? Oh, yes, I was telling you about my first trip on the subway. At first I found everything so overwhelming in the city. I was impressed by the lights, the color and design of the seats, ventilation system, sling bars and above all, the people. People of all social classes dressing in many different ways. São Paulo subway is a melting pot of diversity. Men in suits, others in Bermuda shorts and slippers, children, women in simple clothes and others in fancy dresses, people carrying luggage, shopping bags or schoolbooks. Some people reading books. Some people taking a nap. The vast majority of them, minding their own lives. São Paulo subway is a sample of life, developing under the ground.

I could not be more impressed on arriving in São Paulo. At points the train came up to the surface, I watched the city through the windows, thrilled. Buildings of all sizes, colors and outlines. Cars that appeared to be brought from the factory only hours ago. The gigantic train of steel dove underground again and I wondered where it would go. I had no idea of its final destination. Today I know the subway map by heart.

We finally stepped out of the train, Jailton and me. I had no idea where I was. Leaving the subway station, I was surprised by a quiet neighborhood, very different from downtown where I had been before. It was completely different from the description my friends gave me of São Paulo. They were not wrong though. In the next days I would come to know the real São Paulo, feeling in my skin the shivers that I bet every migrant feels when meeting such a tremendous megalopolis for the first time.

To reach Fábio's home in the east zone of the city, we took a private van, a very common means of conveyance in São Paulo. The van rode for twenty minutes. Then we had to walk for almost ten more minutes. It was five o'clock in the afternoon and cold. The scenery and landscape were no longer glamorous. The high buildings were gone. Cars were all old and patched up. Jailton knew every neighbor and kept saying hello to everyone. I had the impression that I was back inland. This was a small village encrusted inside the big city. I realized why people used to call that place a "village". Let me admit it: this was the first "favela" I lived in. Anyway, here was the house, a place to rest my bones, after a 36-hour journey.

vimeo.com/114743632

Fábio was not home yet. He would not get back from the pet shop until late at night. This time of year is when people take their animals to be made handsome for the holidays. Many people think their pets are entitled to party, too.

I desperately needed a shower. I entered the house with an incredible anxiety. It was a tiny place with just one bedroom and one bathroom. I was wondering where I was going to sleep, since Fábio lived with his sister and a niece. At that moment, I understood Fábio's generosity, having me in a place that hardly sheltered his own family.

Next morning, I said to myself, I would start looking for a job. I could not afford to go on living in a place like that. I had come from a place with plenty of space, even for the poor. My friends tried to warn me about the difficulties I may have to face. They tried to warn me about facing embarrassing situations like occupying a place in a bedroom already used by three persons. I didn't listen to them. Anyway, I could not back-pedal. My pride would not allow me to do that. I heard the phrase again: "You won't stay more than two days in São Paulo".

Definitely not. I would not go back to Bahia defeated.

First night

Fábio came home very late. I had not seen him for six months, since the parties of June. I saw him walking up the street with his strong, handsome, sympathetic smile, which revealed the quality of his soul. He carried a Christmas food basket.

Fábio is one of my best friends. When he got close to me, he made a big smile, kissed my forehead and hugged me. We entered the house. He rushed to take a bath, because he had been dealing with cats and dogs all day. He was eager for any news from home. Then we talked about my situation. He promised to make all efforts to find me a job at the pet shop. He told me that the shop always needed people to wash the animals, an activity that required no experience or knowledge. He also knew some folks in other shops and promised to contact all of them. It was a long talk. In this small space I felt I was intruding. He said that he had bought the house, so I did not have to worry about spending my money on rent. I replied that I did not want to interfere in his family routine, and because of that, I would start looking for another place to live right away. Continuing his generosity, he assured me that I could stay for as long as I needed. "The house is small", he said, "but it is like mother's heart: there is always room for one more".

We ate a marvelous dinner prepared by Lia, Fábio's sister. With his family, I did not feel alone in that "stone jungle".

We prepared to go to bed. I felt that I made everybody uncomfortable and I felt I was inconveniencing them. My presence took away their family privacy. I did not like the situation at all, but there was no immediate solution on the horizon. Nevertheless, I slept like a child. I was exhausted. It was still dark when I woke up. Too many things to think about: a place to live, a job to find. It was urgent to move away. I did not want to be a hindrance to Fábio's family.

Finding a job would certainly be difficult in the middle of the holidays. In January too. But in February it would be a little easier only after the Carnival. I put on my clothes and went out. I needed some fresh air.

I had an idea of calling the person I saw as my second mother, my Aunt Nadir, my mother's sister. The kind of woman who would give her last bit of food to feed someone in need. She lived in São Paulo for quite a while, since the 80s. She surely would help me.

Why did I not look for her as soon as I got to the city? Being my mother's sister, she was one of the people that tried to keep me living in my hometown. Because of that, I saw her as someone who would not support my dreams. As many female migrants who come to São Paulo, she started working as a domestic servant and still does. She knows the difficulties and dangers of the big city.

However, the night I spent in Fábio's place, witnessing his deprivations, opened my eyes. In less than 24 hours, I understood why so many people in Bahia had tried to keep me from coming to São Paulo. OK, each person has a different history. Some people accept opportunities. It was my chance to prove myself a man.

I went back to Fábio's. It was still early in the morning. Nobody was supposed to work that day, because it was a Saturday. We gathered around the table and had a nice breakfast, thanks to the basket that Fábio had brought the night before. For the first time I tried a panettone.

First days

At my mother's suggestion, I had prepared a list with names and telephone numbers of relatives who lived in São Paulo. On that list I found the name of one of my mother's cousins. Much older than my mother, she is called Aunt Vanda by us. I went to the street to find a public phone. In São Paulo these are called "big ears" because of the shape. I dialed Aunt Vanda's number, somewhat anxious. She answered the phone, warm and affectionate as always. I asked to talk to Aunt Nadir; they lived together. I waited with butterflies in my stomach. She finally came, and it seemed to me that she was already expecting my call. She listened very carefully to me explain my situation. I asked if she could help. Concerned she said yes and told me how to find her home. Aunt Vanda and Aunt Nadir's house would be my home for the next three years. It was the second "favela" I lived in. Aunt Vanda owned the house, and Aunt Nadir pays her a rent to help with the expenses. I ran back to Fábio's and told him that I had found a bigger place. He understood, wished me luck and walked me to the bus stop.

I felt as if from that moment I was rowing my own boat.

The two-story house was much bigger. However, five families lived there. Aunt Nadir's part had two bedrooms, one for her and Uncle Alfredo, and the other for their daughter, Nívea. I slept in the living room and felt welcomed. I was safe.

First days in Sao Paulo

vimeo.com/115609941

That first week flew by. Initially I was afraid of going out alone. Moreover, I was homesick. I cried for two days. Luckily, I soon overcame the emotional impact, mainly because my aunt welcomed me into her home. We gathered together for Christmas Eve, celebrating with a barbecue party.

During the week, Fábio called on me and gave me telephone numbers of people from Bahia, living in São Paulo, who might give me a hand in getting work. On December 31, I called Alessandro Rocha. He worked as a dog hairdresser in a fancy pet shop in one of the most important malls in São Paulo. Alessandro later became a very good friend of mine. Today he is married to Tatiana and is the father of Jean Lucca, an excellent soccer player. On the telephone, Alessandro was remarkably positive. He did not know which stores were hiring workers and recommended me to wait to the end of the holidays. He suggested we meet at the shopping center, after his shift. He was going to gather with his colleagues for a year-end party and invited me to join the group; it should be a good opportunity to make contacts. I accepted in the blink of an eye. For three reasons: meet new people, get contacts for a job and have a beer. Oh! How I love beer!

I told Aunt Nadir I was going out with some friends. She worried, because it was going to be my first night out of home and asked if I would know how to get there. I answered: "Use your tongue and you will get to Rome". Today I know that this is true, because I have been to Rome on my travels!

I may sound naive, but I think that meeting was my first act of independence.

At the subway station, I had the notion of what São Paulo really is—a city of social contrasts. There is poverty and right next to it, the second fanciest mall of São Paulo, the Higienopolis Shopping Center, surrounded by wonderful buildings. At the entrance, beautiful people, well dressed, so too, some men strangely dressed, wearing hats. I know now that the neighborhood is an important orthodox Jewish community. Inside, Christmas lights, more nice-looking people celebrating the beginning of a new year. I was literally astonished with everything I saw.

I found Fábio, Alessandro and Robério, Alessandro's youngest brother, my old classmate, and we all went to a bar. Some other fellows showed up and we celebrated the coming of the year 2001. I talked about my journey, my first impressions of the city, and my fears about finding a job quickly. Everybody was sympathetic, because they too have been through the same epic saga. They all promised to tell me if they found a job for me.

After many beers, we left. No one allowed me to share the bill. They knew that I had no job yet and said it was a tradition for newcomers. It happens the same with first-time sailors; they do not pay bills in crew bars until they receive the first wage. I have also done the same myself for several friends. Thank God I did not have to pay, because the money I had was very little.

First panic

We drove to the house of Mrs Cida, mother of Alessandro and Robério. Both my friends were happy. It was a nice party and they had received a good amount of money that day with tips from the customers. I was happy, too, meeting Robério, a friend from my times at school. He was the driver and I remember being amazed by the craziest traffic I had ever seen. How could anyone drive in traffic like that? People crossed the streets, walking amongst the cars. Seeing my friend driving with great skill made me very proud of him. They told me that the traffic was not so bad that day, because of the holidays.

For my peace of mind, the ride was short, less than five miles. They lived near the Museum of the University of São Paulo, in a neighborhood called Ipiranga. In the house lived a big family: Cida, Salvador and five kids, all of them born in Boninal. It was love at first sight. All the family received me in a wonderful way and I felt very welcome. The table was laid with nice food and the house full of cheerfulness. My friends opened the wine bottles that they got as gifts from the pet shop customers. Each sip made me mellow and confident, feeling safe in a big house, surrounded by merry fellows, in a fine neighborhood. Every little thing was magic.

Alessandro had recommended to me to take some spare clothes, so I was ready to stay with them for the night. But somebody remembered that a big New Year's Eve party was prepared at a major avenue of the city, the Paulista Avenue, with a show of my favorite band Asa de Águia (Eagle's Wing). I was excited with the thought of seeing the show. As I was already at ease with my friends, I convinced Alessandro to take me to that party. He promptly agreed. Everybody in the family tried to dissuade us from going downtown, because of the gathering crowds and the risk of riots. Mrs Cida advised us to stay home. We should have listened to her, because a mother's heart is always right. I will explain.

By the time Alessandro and I left, it was already past eleven at night. We took a bus and less than 15 minutes later we got off in front of the subway station Paraíso, the beginning of Paulista Avenue. The bus could not go any further because the streets were closed for cars. So we walked, rushing to reach the show in time. The avenue was incredibly crowded, with maybe more than one million people. We could hear but not see the band. It took us ten more minutes to get in front of the stage. It was almost midnight. Most people were wearing white clothes, as a symbol of peace, but not us. Maybe this was our mistake…

While we waited for the countdown to the year 2001, a fight started near us. Members of some gang did not like "Axé Music", and begun to throw bottles and cans to the stage. The vocalist Durval Lelis tried, in vain, to calm the crowd. He interrupted the show, because he was afraid of what might happen. His decision was the straw that broke the camel's back. The fight spread and I could not run to escape. People pushed me around. I received a punch from I do not know who.

Could there be anything worse than this? Yes, there could!

My friend and I tried to escape by going to the rear of the stage. We could not make it through. The military police shock troops were coming towards us, spraying pepper spray in the air and throwing flash grenades behind us, a group dressed in black launched bottles against the police officers. We were trapped in the middle. Paulista Avenue turned into a battleground. It was midnight and, while everyone else celebrated, we were stuck between two groups fighting. I was desperate. Finally, thanks to the effort of a bunch of people not involved in the conflict, we managed to get through down the safety handrails and run away.

I was safe then, right? Wrong!

Alessandro ran in the direction of the subway station but I ran in the opposite direction. I did not know where I was. At a safe distance, I looked back and did not see my friend. I froze. What now? I did not know his home address, phone number or the name of the bus to catch to get there. I was lost. Without seeing any other alternative, I went back to the middle of the conflict, trying to keep a safe distance. Almost everybody was wearing white clothes, so I thought that Alessandro's checkered shirt would be easy to find. I had several minutes of real terror. All of a sudden, someone touched my shoulder. I turned, terrified, ready to defend myself from the troublemakers. Relief: it was Alessandro, my savior. We did not have time to hug. We ran away and practically dove into a taxi. Tired as hell, we could not even tell the driver the address where we wanted to go. By that time there were no buses anymore. This was indeed a flagrant failure of São Paulo urban mobility plan; public transportation does not keep up with the city's rhythm. Those people who live at the periphery and suburbs cannot really count on public transportation to enjoy the activities going on in the city center. The taxi driver took us for robbers escaping from the police and refused the ride. We had to get out, walk a few more blocks and then find another taxi.

The way back home was fast. In the house, everybody was still celebrating. They had turned the TV off, so had not heard about the problem at Paulista Avenue. We told them everything, shivering. Seeing us unharmed, they started making fun of us. The night ended happily, but we kept that trauma with us for a quite some time.

The year 2001 began, as I remember, with strong emotions but a hard lesson now learnt.

Chapter 5

Dreaming

In this chapter I am going to write more about my hometown, so you, the reader, can understand a little better the place I came from and, consequently, who I am.

After I left Boninal, in the first hours of the bus trip, I kept thinking about my life and the expectations I had in relation to São Paulo. I was euphoric but, at the same time, already homesick. The 1200 miles of the journey were fundamental for me to organize my expectancies. Even though the arrival at that crowded bus terminal impressed me much, I felt lonely, small and lost. Only when I saw Fábio coming from work did I calm down. He represented, at that moment, the possibility of beginning a new life. I followed my way. He followed his. After three years, destiny reserved a grateful surprise: the privilege of sharing an apartment with him and my friend João Reis. That was another and very important beginning. I feel obliged to give, in this book, warm thanks to my friend Fábio.

I have to admit, although quite ashamed, that I had a certain distaste for studying. São Paulo forced me to change my ideas about education. I wished to make money and be part of society. I was working a thankless job without prospects, I could not keep doing that. I do not have anything against manual labor, which can be as dignified as any other work, but my dreams were different. I wanted something else. However, with the kind of education I had at that time, the most I could hope for, was to save money to buy a car and half a dozen pieces of clothing.

Being motivated towards my goals, I thought about this. I reached the conclusion that learning English and getting a high school certificate must be my immediate goal in life. Some of you may think that those are very trivial achievements, but for me, a lad who once dreamed of being a soccer player, these represented a jump higher than the London Eye. The English language became to me the golden key that would open the door of knowledge, then the doors to the world. I would see places, I would meet people, and I would see different cultures, a richness that nobody can take away from me. I respect all dreams. I think that Brazil would be a better and more equal society if everyone put education as their life goal. I feel that I can say this because I am now a kind of representative of a social stratum that earns many good things because of education. Education allows me to value the world even more.

Boy from the "Down Street"

For a boy so simple, like me, born and raised in the Bahia inland, the verb *travel* always represented a great desire. When I was a kid, I had the dream of knowing places like Bom Jesus da Lapa—Good Lord of the Cave, 200 miles away from my home—and, perhaps, Salvador, the Bahia state capital. Moreover, and hopefully, the most unreachable utopia of all: São Paulo. At that time, São Paulo was far more distant from my place than London is today at eleven hours away by plane.

I think of Madam Dona, the most famous midwife in Boninal. She was the first person who saw me, even before my mother laid her protective eyes on me. Dona, certainly, praised the heaven for me to become a healthy happy boy. A good man, fundamentally. I believe I am a good man, and I wished I had had a chance to tell her about things I saw throughout the world. Even though I know that, for her, the Leaning Tower of Pisa is nothing more than a crooked building.

Down Street, the area where I was born and grew up, will always be in my memories. The place is magically simple. In fact, it is a set of streets united by alleys, by the banks of the River Cochó. The name of this quarter is symbolized in its social condition. In the low part of the town lived the less socially favored; in the high part, Up Street, lived the richer inhabitants.

There was a clear social and geographic division in my childhood. During the soccer matches the boys from Down Street would meet up, trying to beat the boys from Up Street. I still remember the first big confrontation between both teams. It was the inauguration of our team jerseys, but the sport shirts did not help us. We lost by the score of 13 to 1. Today I thank our adversaries for not demanding us to swap shirts as the unwritten rule recommends. Our team improved with the passing of time. We were compelled to improve, because it was unbearable to hear the mocking we received from everyone who knew the score. It is a shame that I do not have a single photo of that marvelous team. We were poor and could not afford a camera. None of us used soccer shoes, so we played barefoot and our toes suffered. At least, we had the jerseys!

Besides soccer, we used to play other games. It was a pleasant time and I could write a book to tell specifically about these games. Nevertheless, let me stay focused.

I have a passion for images and photography. My collection today is more than 40,000 photographs. This interest I certainly developed from watching Luizão, Big Louie, the photographer. As a boy I sat every afternoon in front of the community black and white TV set in the middle of the town square, enchanted by the images.

We were happy, even with the many difficulties we faced, especially for a family that did not have a father to support them. I remember my anxiety when Aunt Nadir, already living in São Paulo, arrived in Boninal with a small TV set that she had brought on her lap on her bus trip. It had a bunch of dials and buttons that I did not know what they were for. It was only possible to tune one channel; to watch cartoons, movies and soap operas. I was excited by the American movies I saw. I never expected to visit the factory of fantasy ... Hollywood!

I climbed a step in the social ladder because my family had a TV set. Some people flattered me while other people envied me. The enthusiasm soon faded and we went back to our street games. Those games were indeed fundamental to our development. No man is an island. No one would grow alone. That is why all the people of my childhood and adolescence, each one in their way, were and still are important for my history.

My history is similar to the history of many of my soccer mates on the banks of the River Cochó. In fact, we had everything lining up to be social delinquents, because we skipped classes to play and lived life as if it were a huge amusement park. Fortunately, for me and for many others, everything turned out very different from what appeared to be our destiny. Today, looking back, I see that most of those boys have succeeded in different ways. From that bunch of kids I know lawyers, teachers, and tradesmen, even a doctor. We contradicted the miserable logics and likely outcome of our origins. All of us improved our lot because of the education that we sought later in life.

I am reminded of my childhood every time I am wandering somewhere in the world. The new and enchanting places we visit take me back to how different they are from my hometown. It was there anyhow, I prepared myself to go to São Paulo. In São Paulo my dreams began flourishing. Wandering the world was one of those dreams.

There was a guy, back in Boninal, with a lot of nicknames. Fatty, for example; I always called him Te. He owned a VW van and earned his living driving groups to tourist places in Bahia. Those trips were like an embryo of the travels I would make later in my life. The difference was that, at that time, my dreams were modest.

There was a woman, Nicinha, whose business was to organize pilgrimages to Bom Jesus da Lapa in July, a month before the party of the patron saint. She still does this, roaming in the town with a notebook and a pen in her hands

to enroll people on her trips. Thanks to her, I went to Bom Jesus da Lapa for six years in a row, between 1994 and 1999. By then I already had a camera and could take lots of photos.

I could mention many other men and women who marked my first period of life. Many of them pushed and shaped me without me even knowing. I remember that morning in December, at the Boninal bus stop, when I heard "You won't last two days in São Paulo". This fellow helped me with this. A challenge, and I thank him every day, but he does not know and perhaps will never know. Before leaving Boninal one of my brother's friends trying to scare me also said that "You won't last two days in Sao Paulo" because for us in the northeast Sao Paulo means a very big thing. If you don't have anybody there or if you have a quiet life back in your village it is considered better not to leave, that's how most there think. For this guy I was cheating my brother leaving, because I had a comfortable life back in Boninal. So he did say that and it hurt me, that's why I never forget it. This is a very common warning given to youngsters before leaving Boninal or other small villages.

In life, in order to live, achieve and prosper we have to take risks. I do take them.

São Paulo represents, for people from the north-eastern inland, a challenge. I have come to know that everything depends on the way we look at it. For me, it was a land of opportunities. Even though I may have stumbled, I did not fall in the beginning. I persisted. I studied. I grew. I arrived there as a Down Street boy, with baggage full of "no" and "I can't". I had to discover and achieve the "yes" and "I can". And so I did.

The boy from Down Street

□ □ □ □ □ □ □

vimeo.com/114837263

Chapter 6

First job, crazy life

Forty days after I arrived in São Paulo, I started the first real and registered job of my life. I already told you that I worked with my brother in Boninal, but that was not a professional relationship. By this I mean that he never worried about filling-in my labor card and registering my work with the state authority.

My first day at work was one of the happiest days I had in São Paulo. Money was flying away in bus and subway tickets. I had spent most of my US$150. Apart from the lack of cash, everything else was fine. I was in love with the city and remain so to this day. I was adopted—and I adopted—a lovely family: warm Aunt Nadir, handy Uncle Alfredo and cousin Nívea.

Uncle Alfredo was very helpful in my search for a job. He guided me and showed me around. He worked as a valet in a car-parking place downtown, at the famous crossing of Rio Branco Avenue and São João Avenue. That parking place still exists. Uncle Alfredo took me with him, so I could see his place of work. He wanted me to get to know the city center, which would then make it easier to look for a job.

The first time I accompanied him I put on my "party outfit", as we say in Bahia. We took a crowded van. Then we took a subway train, which was crowded as well. It was early in the morning, the first business day after the holidays, and I could see the city in its regular routine. I will never forget my feelings, amongst the multitude of people that literally dragged me around as if I was a twig floating in the ocean. We got off at a subway station two blocks away from Uncle's workplace. We got there a few minutes before nine o'clock, just when the executives of the buildings nearby were arriving with their fancy cars. He immediately started working and I stepped aside and watched, dazzled by the spectacular cars coming to that gigantic parking place. All of that looked like a dream to me. I was imagining myself driving one of those cars when reality called me back to Earth. My goal was to find a job and help Aunt Nadir to pay the rent. She had never mentioned anything about it, but I considered it my duty to contribute.

Uncle Alfredo advised me to go to the news-stand nearby. It is common, in São Paulo, for news-stands to stick the pages of "want ads" up on one of the side-walls. This meant that people could check the ads before buying the newspapers. I walked in the direction of the news-stand without much hope, but when I got there, I saw a lot of ads. I took my time to check them one by one. All the ads asked for previous experience or at least a high school diploma. I was sad and frustrated because there was no place for me as a 21 year old, new in town and without a diploma. What should I do?

I saw people forming a line right by the side of the news-stand. It was an enormous line, with people of all ages. With nothing else to do, I decided to join them in line and asked the guy next to me what the line was about. He explained that they were waiting for an interview with an employment agency. There were, he said, situations vacant in many areas. I told him about my lack of experience. He reassured me that some of the job offers did not require experience. Well, I had all my documents, so I decided to wait and see what was going to happen. After almost one hour, finally it was my turn to fill in the form. In order to do that, I had to take the elevator, also a new experience for me. The employment agency was located at the 14th floor. The elevator's ascent caused a cold sensation in my belly—maybe it was anxiety. I got out trembling and nervous. All the people at the agency seemed far more prepared than I was. Filling in the job request form, I looked slyly to my side to check what the others were writing, so I would not do anything wrong. I soon realized that the task was easy: just note down my personal information. I left blank the sections about position and wage. I handed my request and was told to wait. Moments later, a very sympathetic girl called me. She read my request and asked why I had not given information about the position I was interested in. I answered, practically confessing my whole history. Perhaps I thought I could be able to stir her heart. It seemed to work, or maybe her job was to pretend to be moved by everyone's history. She told me that there were some positions for commission sales personnel that did not require experience or a diploma. However, she was very honest, by telling me that I would have as competitors some people much more experienced than me, and they probably would be chosen. She practically convinced me to give up the position. However, I insisted so she advised me to think it over for 15 days and then come back to let her know if I really wanted the job.

It was not an encouraging experience. I went back to the ground floor by the stairs, walked to the parking place and spent the rest of the day in thought.

As days went by, one third of my money vanished. I paid US$2.50 a day to buy bus and subway tickets to go to the region where Uncle Alfredo worked. That place was the only place I knew. I was afraid to go anywhere else and get lost. Moreover, Uncle Alfredo was very optimistic and persuaded me to go there, and I trusted his instinct. I ate out of the lunch-box my aunt prepared for me. When I needed to visit any other place I now walked. At the weekends I stayed home. Even so, my money was almost spent and I had not found a job. I was feeling terrible, without any desire to visit friends. I used the telephone of Aunt Vanda to make a few calls in an attempt to find work. It was the only telephone in the vicinity. Most of the calls were in vain, but one of them was special.

I realized that the only thing I knew was driving. So I called my friend Alzetim, in Boninal, to ask the number of his cousin Alexandro, my former colleague in the soccer matches. I knew he was the manager of a parking place located near the Paulista Avenue and I intended to offer my services. Alzetim did not know the phone number but gave me the address of Multipark ... at least I thought I heard him say Multipark. I looked on the map and the next day, after leaving Uncle Alfredo at his work, I walked to the address. I found Augusta Street, walked all the way along it but nothing! I started all over again, asked here and there, but nobody knew Multipark, Alexandro or anything that gave a clue to my search. Finally, somebody said that, at the parallel street, Haddock Lobo, there were some parking places. I walked on again, but this time amazed by the beauty of the neighborhood and the nice architecture of the houses, the sumptuousness of the shops. Nevertheless, I found no parking place whatsoever. Much later, I would discover that the name of the parking place where Alexandro works is Evonpark!

I was ready to give up my search. Almost at the corner of the Paulista Avenue, I stopped. Right in front of me, a magnificent building rose up. It was the Marriott's Renaissance Hotel. For some minutes, I enjoyed the view of elegant people moving around, entering fancy cars, prettier than those I had seen in the parking place where my uncle worked. The employees wore impeccable uniforms and their faces were happy. I stood amazed. I gawked actually. Then I noticed a security guard scowl at me. I was frightened, as if I had done something wrong just by being there, so I left.

Audacity

vimeo.com/114745691

Do not consider it a cliché or a fairy tale what I am about to tell you. When I saw that building, I said, "I will work there, one day". I went back to the parking place, feeling down-and-out. Nevertheless, I had found some compensation by getting to know that nice neighborhood. I had been thirty days in São Paulo, with only a few bucks left in my pocket. I had no hope to cheer my soul. I did not know then that my first job was very close. Once again trying to help, Alfredo told me about another parking place that was often in need of valets. I went checking and found out that the forms could be filled-in on Mondays, between nine and twelve o'clock. So, on a cloudy Monday of January 22nd 2001, wearing my best clothes, I showed up in the parking place to ask about applying for a job. Mário, the man in charge, received me with sympathy. He was tall, with very well combed blond hair and a strong Italian accent. At first, I was so nervous that I could not understand him. I carefully listened to his instructions and answered all the questions. After a long conversation, I managed to convince him of my driving skills, even though I had only a provisional license. He informed me that I had been approved and that I should arrange the documentation and medical examinations to start working on the first day of February.

It is difficult to express how I felt. I went back singing to the parking place to give Uncle Alfredo the news. It was good fortune for everybody. For me, however, it was much more than that. It was my independence. Today, every February 1st, wherever I am, I take a minute to say thanks and remember the joy that job meant to me—a new beginning.

First job

The parking place was also a car wash facility. My shift started at midday and ended at eleven at night. But for my first day of work I was too anxious to wait. I took a bus around 10:00am and, during the route, I looked at my labor card again and again, to check my wage: R$399,90 (then about US$170 a month).

It was a Thursday. I arrived there by ten thirty in the morning, well before my scheduled time. I was somewhat worried. What would my workmates be like? What about the clients? What challenges would I meet in the job? Would it be difficult to drive those cars?

I presented myself to the supervisor, Roberto. A well educated, tall and fat man. He wore glasses and all the time re-arranged them, as they slid down his nose. He introduced me to the three people who were going to be my new co-workers. Like me, Maria the cashier and Rivaldo the valet had come from the Northeast. Claudionor was the administrator. Roberto let us know that he would pass by several times per day to collect the money and cash. As soon as he left my colleagues overloaded me with questions: where did I come from, where had I worked before, did I really know how to drive. At that moment, the first car appeared and they asked me to park it. They were trying to test me of course. With everybody's eyes on me, I was nervous. But I did OK, because the parking place had plenty of space and there were no

My first job - car park attendant

lamp posts in the way. My colleagues, Maria, Rivaldo and Claudionor smiled at me and Claudionor even paid me a compliment. They also gave me advice. That I should always look back instead of using the rear-view mirrors, that I should always apply the park brake and that I should check both sides before opening the doors. I had gained their confidence. Because of that confidence from that time on I was the only one parking the cars. As excuses, they said they were tired or were working longer than I was. I never minded, eager as I was to drive those new cars with different controls. It was a party for me and I worked joyfully.

One day, a car arrived, and my workmates knew it well. The car had an automatic transmission. They knew that I had come from inland where things are poorer and perhaps had never seen a car like that. So they decided to have some fun with me. They waited for the owner to leave and told me to park the car. They did not know, however, that Uncle Alfredo taught me how to drive an automatic car. Even though they were annoyed, I won their respect. I felt proud of myself, but pretended that I did not notice anything.

On pay-day, at the beginning of March, I withdrew US$50 and handed the money to Aunt Nadir, as my contribution towards the rent. She tried to refuse but I could not let her do that. My self-esteem improved quite a lot after that. A week later, I received my first checkbook. What a glorious feeling! I remembered watching my brother signing checks to pay suppliers, and considered it a great achievement to be able to now do so myself. I also received a credit card. A damned credit card!

First night out

After ninety days of work, I passed my probation period. By then I was friends with everybody in the company. The administrator, the skinny Claudionor, was a night owl. Not by chance he had three kids, each one from a different mother. He was also a motor biker. I had a motorbike with the nickname of *Lacraia*, which means centipede. I will tell more about it later. That night, Claudionor and I decided to go out for a beer, to celebrate. Things, however, did not work well for me.

It was a Friday, the most effervescent night in Sao Paulo, and we planned to go to a dancing place where the hit was the *forró*, which is a typical Brazilian north-eastern dance. I had to work the next morning, starting at seven, but

I was happy, with money in my pocket… what the heck? Moreover, going out at night was nothing new for me. Just across the street, there was an unpretentious bar. We entered there first, to drink something and warm up, because certainly the price of beverage would be much higher in the dancing place. We ordered two beers. It was my first time in São Paulo at night—since the riot—and I felt a little shy, observing the drunkards and feeling sorry for them. Before I knew it, we were on our third beer, accompanied by a shot of whiskey. Well, after all, a person who walks out in the rain surely gets wet! We talked and we drank. Hours went by and many drinks went down the hatch. By five in the morning, I was more than merry. I was very tired and decided to go home. The sun was rising, spilling light over the neighborhood. I climbed onto the bike, dreaming of my bed, and suddenly remembered that I was supposed to be at work in less than two hours. I panicked. In two hours I could not go home and come back in time. The alternative was to go to the parking place and take a nap before starting work. I asked Claudionor to accompany me and talk to the night valet, who did not know me, to let me sleep in the underground garage. Claudionor was the boss so surely the night valet would not refuse to do him a favor. He did, luckily the valet helped me, and Claudionor left.

There was only one chair available. This meant I had to sit in the staircase, which was at the underground level. I asked my colleague to wake me up at 6:40, and I tried to sleep. I barely could rest, because I felt uncomfortable and feared to oversleep. The guy indeed woke me up in time and I got up to work, counting the cars and checking the cash. He said goodbye and left me alone. I took a walk, checked that everything was all right with the cars and I entered the cabin. In there, I found a chair and finally sat in something soft. I was so tired that I thought the chair was a beloved girlfriend embracing me. It warmed my body and my heart and I fell in love with that chair. I fell asleep as well. I woke at around ten o'clock, to the screams of an unfriendly Portuguese man. It took me a while to understand that he was yelling at me. He was talking to someone on his cell phone and pointing his finger in my direction. I was in a daze and had no idea what was going on.

A few minutes later, Roberto, my supervisor, arrived and explained to me that the Portuguese fellow was the owner. The world collapsed on my head. I had heard about how rude the man was. He yelled some more and then went away. Roberto saw my predicament and told me that he was going to have to get somebody to replace me, but I assured him that such a big scare would keep me from sleeping again. Roberto even chuckled softly at my desperate joke and warned me that he would not punish me because that was my first failure. Even so he said that on Monday we should have a talk. I did not relax until two o'clock in the afternoon, when somebody came to relieve me.

On Monday, instead of getting a scolding, I was mocked. Everybody laughed at me because I was caught sleeping by Mr Ferreira and because I had been a victim of Claudionor who was well known as the night owl and administrator. Evidently every now and then he chose someone to get blind drunk with. The one lesson was sufficient for me.

The "centipede" bike

Through the influence of my brother, in Bahia, I already liked motorbikes very much. With my second wage in the parking place, and counting on the "fantastic" credit facilities offered by my new best friend, the bank, I managed to buy a used Honda 1988 bike from a cousin. To close the deal, I cashed money up to the credit card limit kindly granted by the bank. This cousin, Dorinho, was a car and bike dealer. He is the type of vendor that makes you buy things that you do not need. In other words he is a very talented salesperson. He assured me that the bike was in perfect condition and that all documentation was correct and as required. I naively believed him and bought the bike without seeing it. I gave myself an excuse to buy the bike. I said to myself that it would reduce the time between home and work. I know now that what I really wanted to do was to be able to buy an important possession myself.

On Sunday, I traveled the city to pick up my new bike. I trusted Dorinho because I learned in my hometown that a handshake is far worthier than a contract. Also the bike was red, a color that I love. I would find out, unfortunately, that he assembled the bike with old spare parts of other bikes. Luckily the documentation was OK!

One day at the end of my shift I got on my bike to go home. I decided to pass by a woodland. All of a sudden, one of the suspensions broke. The net I used to carry my raincoat got hooked in the spokes of the wheel and snapped the chain. I almost fell, but managed to control the bike and jumped off. It was close to midnight and there was no one around to help. I had no choice but to push the bike the many kilometers home. On the way, I cursed my cousin a thousand times and made a decision to never ride that bike again.

It could have been God's message. Later on I made a deal with a truck driver I knew to deliver that bike to my brother in Boninal. Denilton received the bike and documentation and sold it. I never knew who bought the bike.

Extra work duties

Once approved in the probation period, everything improved for me. I was friendly and polite with the clients and colleagues and they liked me. Wanting more money and following the recommendation of a friend, I started looking for extra work in other car parks outside of my usual work hours. I was single and my nights and mornings were all free. Soon I started working night shifts. I worked hard and was able to save money and even get some amusement. That allowed me to get to know new people. The problem was that I finished working late at night and could not go home. The alternative was sleeping on old mattresses in the parking place. Besides serving as a valet, I also washed and polished cars, earning some extra money. I was obsessed with the idea of buying a newer bike. Six months later I bought a nice one. I rode it for quite a while but mainly for going back home after work. At the end of the year 2001, I bought another bike that was a nearly new one.

I could write a book about everything that happened to me during this first job but I want to move forward with my story so I can show how discipline, work and belief in oneself are worth having.

Moving ahead

My "divorce" from my first workplace was signed on January 28th, 2002. Everything was settled in a conversation with the same person who had hired me, Mário, partner and son-in-law of Mr Ferreira. By coincidence, the conversation took place in the same spot where Mr Ferreira had surprised me sleeping.

Resigning from my work came about because by now I was homesick. In my telephone calls to my family, I knew that there was no longer resentment about the fact that I had left for Sao Paulo and so I could go back and meet with my family and relatives. I knew though, that the boss would not give me a vacation. Therefore, I decided to quit the job. In one year by working hard I had been able to buy three motorbikes. But, I was still tied to a mediocre job because I had not completed high school. In fact, what I intended was to spend the Carnival in Boninal showing off my professional achievements.

I proposed a deal to Mário, in order to evade labor laws and release the company of fines for dismissal without just cause. He accepted, warning me that it was a company policy not to re-admit a dismissed employee. I answered that I was going to invest the money I had saved in a new business in my hometown. I said this only to justify my resignation. All legal procedures fulfilled, I went shopping to buy gifts for everyone and then took a bus to make the return trip to my family home. I had a large suitcase, a pocket full of money and a soul filled with serenity.

So there I was once again in my field of daisies. My new bike, taken by the same truck driver, was waiting for me. My brother reserved one of his cars for my use. This was amazing as he had never before allowed me even a short ride on his bike! It was the best Carnival party of my life. My family was happy. I wore new clothes all the time, spending money earned from my so longed for independence. However, as the saying goes, nothing lasts forever.

The Carnival passed by. The parties passed by. The money passed by. Sixty days later, I began to feel uneasy in my hometown, living the same way, each day with less money. It was time to go back to São Paulo. I already knew the "stepping stones", how to get there and where to go. I also knew, however, that it was not going to be easy to find a new job. Anyway, I had to leave Boninal again. So I did in April 2002.

Chapter 7

Daring to think big

I may say that in my life, thank God, circles are completed and new ones begin.

Well, there I was, like an oscillating wave, back in São Paulo. Once more unemployed, but this time because of my own carelessness. At least by now I had some experience and my attitude was more positive.

I repeated my steps and went back to Aunt Nadir's house. I still had five parcels of the unemployment insurance benefit to receive so I could help with the rent. In my mind, it was enough money to keep me going for five months. How foolish I was! In fact, I had nothing. No high school diploma, no professional experience, and no future. Even so, I decided to go back to Boninal in June, for the Saint John's party. Which indeed, I did.

I really do not know why I did this. Perhaps to show off a bit more. Or maybe trying to crown my "achievements" by winning the love of a woman. The practical question, anyway, was that Fábio and Robério decided to go by car to Boninal. However, Fábio did not know how to drive and so I was asked to join them and share the steering wheel. I guess the opportunity put two things together: my wandering spirit and my irresponsibility.

Therefore, in order not to compromise my next trip home, I decided not to work with a registered labor card in the meantime. I had my unemployment insurance, after all!

Anyway, I got a job as a plumber's assistant, in fact a mason assistant, in a company owned by a man I knew in Bahia. It was a hard task, especially because I had to get up at 5 o'clock everyday. My duties were taking care of water pipes in buildings and houses in many regions of the city. I assisted the plumber João whose nickname was Borrela. He was a short man and very sweet in nature. He also stuttered, maybe because of his angry wife. João's mood, at work, depended much on what happened the night before, at home. I met his wife once, when I helped the family to move to another home in an old Chevette. This story deserves to be told.

João Borrela did not know how to drive. He was a man of great qualities, polite, an excellent plumber, hard worker, punctual, disciplined. He could not drive though. Because of this handicap of João's, the company owners bought an old Chevette and promoted me to the position of "chauffeur". In fact, I served both functions: plumber assistant and driver. João and I made a fine work duo. In the first week, as a demonstration of confidence, the bosses allowed me to take the car home one night. I lived about 20 miles away from my job. All went well on the way home. However, the following morning, very early and still dark, I got in the Chevette and headed to my work place. In a very crowded avenue, I stopped behind another car to wait for a traffic light to go green. Suddenly, I heard a terrible metallic noise and felt a shake. An old woman, inattentive, had come with her lustrous shiny car and crashed in the rear of my car. The impact pushed the Chevette against the car in front. Damn! First day using the company's car and I was turned into sandwich stuffing! Fortunately, I didn't get hurt. The woman admitted her fault and promised to pay for the damages. She kept her promise. I had to explain the incident to the boss. Very nervous, I told him what had happened. He understood, but I never took that car home again. For some time I felt insecure when driving but I was the company driver, so I had to keep driving. That was my first accident in São Paulo's traffic. I would face some more and I will write about those later in this book.

I have gone through other difficult moments in the company but everything came out all right. I made good friends there. During that period, I felt how detrimental it was to not have studied. I circulated in the noble neighborhoods of the city. One day João and I were breaking the kitchen wall of a fancy apartment to repair a pipe. The lady started yelling at me, reproaching me because I was making too much dirt in the kitchen. She repeated this every five minutes. She was so annoying that I could not avoid saying: "I should have listened to my mother. I did not study and because of this I am obliged to listen to you talking to me like that!" The woman agreed!

The curious thing was that saying this gave me an immediate sensation of assuredness. I continued to work—or make a mess, as the client said—without paying attention to her complaints. It was then, at that very moment, that I decided to go back to school. That woman had a tremendous influence in my decision to become the person I am today. But she will never know that, or that I am grateful!

Party, party

As planned, in June I quit my two jobs and left for 15 days of partying, in Boninal. I felt as if by driving, I could pay back Fábio's generosity in receiving me into his home when I first came to São Paulo. In addition, I insisted that he and Robério stay in my family house, in Boninal, because their families lived very far from the center of the town. My mother offered lunch to both of them, with the typical generosity of the inland people. It was almost a banquet. I did not need to say how happy I was in seeing my friends and family together.

During the 15 nights, my friends and I had a wonderful time, spending money and chasing girls. During those days, I thought of the steps I should take when back in São Paulo.

At the same bar where Fábio and I talked about life in São Paulo two years earlier, I met a great friend called João Reis. Guess what—he had similar thoughts! Even with some other friends at the table, João preferred to talk to me. In the first place, because he had no sympathy for Fábio, considering him a snob and not very sociable. His impression would change later and I will tell you how. Secondly, João Reis saw me as a friend who had gone south and succeeded. He wanted my opinion about his moving to São Paulo.

It was an irony of destiny. It was now my turn to tell someone the same things I did not like to hear. At the same time though, I told him that São Paulo does have opportunities. Of course, I did my best to keep him dreaming, but I mentioned all the difficulties that I had to cope with. Less than twenty days after our conversation João Reis arrived in São Paulo.

Tragic return

The party was over. We drove back to São Paulo. That day, July 7th, 2002, we gathered in Mrs Cida's house to celebrate Robério's birthday. We heard the news in the middle of the party. My great friend Leandro Castro back at home, with whom I had been feasting less than a week before, had suffered a motorbike accident and died. Unfortunately, there would not be time to go back for the funeral. The only thing I could do was pray for him. I confess that Boninal became a sadder place in my memory after his death.

São Paulo, however, is implacable. There, we have no time to think about life or mourn death. I had to get back to work.

Thinking big now

August, the month of my birthday of the year 2002, I would receive a job that, once again, would twist my trajectory. What job? Valet, again.

I tried my luck in a place that, for me, was like an oasis in the desert of my dreams. That building I saw when I was navigating in search of my first boat, in São Paulo—the Renaissance São Paulo Hotel. To work in a hotel of the Marriott Company would be more than just independence. It would represent prestige, financial settlement, and security.

Self-assured, if not pretentious, after one year in São Paulo I felt experienced enough to apply for a job in that hotel. I went there one day to ask about the conditions of application. They told me that they would interview only the first fifty persons in line on a certain date. At the scheduled date I borrowed Robério's clothes, in order to look a little smarter. I was feeling very confident until I saw the others in line, outside the hotel. All of them well dressed and perfumed. I trembled, nervous, inspecting each in the line. When my turn came my nervousness ended and a strong desire to work there came over me. The place smelled brand new, each smallest thing in its place, not a single spot of dirt could be seen, not one spot on the shiny floor. The structure was gigantic. The environment was imposing. I filled in the application form as required for a position of valet. My turn for the interview arrived. The girl was very kind and I almost fell in love with her! We talked for a few minutes and gradually I gained confidence because I fulfilled all the requirements. I mean … almost all! Then she asked me about my high school diploma. Embarrassed, I responded that I did not have a diploma. She explained that the company demanded at least the high school diploma for every candidate. It was a cold shower. So close to the job but I could not get it because I did not finish my studies. Even so, I left the place convinced that I would one day definitely work there. First, though, I would have to finish my studies.

But, even before that, I had to get a job. My money was running out!

Chapter 8

Money cannot buy friendship

In São Paulo, contradicting the saying that this city is a cold and unfriendly place, I reconnected with old friends and met new ones.

I went looking for my friend Alexandre Nunes, a former work colleague. He was working in a car park cooperative. I asked about the job, filled in a form—I was getting good at it—and I was hired!

Let me explain how a cooperative works. They hire valets, cashiers, administrators, etc. and so operate as outsource suppliers to companies. They are set up this way so they won't have to pay work incumbencies in the form of sick leave and holidays and other usual employee benefits. It was a fine arrangement for the client companies because it kept costs very low. However, later, some employees claimed their rights in the Labor Courts, and the cooperative fell apart. In the meantime, I had a flexible schedule and could work with Robério in the pet shop "Bad Dog" during the weekends. He had talked about me and his boss accepted me as a commissioned worker to bathe the pets on Thursdays, Fridays and Saturdays. For a few months, I worked double shifts.

At the cooperative, as a beginner, I had few duties. We were paid by the hour. For small events there were the "shock troops", a select group. For me, I worked night events on the weekends, which no other employee wanted to do. It was better for me because I needed to juggle two jobs. I was assigned to attend events in hotels, and one of them was really special for me. It was the Renaissance Hotel. Less than three months after being rejected, I was back there parking the cars of clients who attended the Renaissance Theater. Many times I worked all day long in the pet shop and then ran to the hotel for the night shift.

The hotel has a gigantic ramp to the underground garage that I had to walk, down and up, many times per night. It was a lot of exercise for me, but I was 23 years old and full of energy. I was happy at that time, but not completely happy. In fact, I still wanted to be a hotel employee. Mainly because they enjoyed some perks that we did not. What pleased me most was the hotel restaurant, where they allowed us to eat. I was used to a modest lunch-box from home; when I saw the variety and abundance of food available at lunchtime or breakfast, I went crazy. Desserts were the same as I saw in the movies—such marvelous ice creams. There was even a soft-drink vending machine that I had never seen anything like before. Each day I was more certain of my desire to work there. But, in order to do that, I had to study.

And so, the year of 2002 went by, a year of many passions. Not only because of the job and the company but also in sentimental terms. I fell in love with a Japanese woman. The romance though did not end as it happens in the movies! Let me tell you.

I used to go often to the same nightclub. First, I went with a couple of friends. Then I became a regular because I liked it and the kind of music they played. I have already written about the precarious public transport in São Paulo, so at night, I normally went by foot. But one night I convinced Alessandro to drive me there in his green Volkswagen. The place was incredibly crowded. Restrooms were not enough for the number of people. Drinks were expensive. The place cost too much for what it offered. But I was quite happy to be there.

After the band played, the crowd calmed down and it was possible to talk with the girls. I decided to dance. Forgive me for this, but it is something I did, and I think still do, quite well. Then I saw those almond-eyes. In the northeast part of Brazil there are no Japanese people. I walked over to the girl and invited her to dance. She accepted and I felt like I was rescuing the princess from the clutches of an evil dragon. During the dance, we talked about our work, our preferences, and our likes and dislikes. Her name was Débora and I will never forget such a beautiful name. As I will never forget the trophy that I conquered during that dance: a warm wet kiss. Those lips made me fall instantaneously in love. On my way back home, I could not stop talking about the princess kiss. Alessandro was bored, hearing me talking so much about her.

With Débora, I shared six months of complete joy. I learned a lot with that pretty girl. She was a wonderful companion. We went out and had fun. We had such harmony in the relationship that I managed to overcome the feeling of inferiority I had had. At her place, I tried for the first time an Asian dish, the yakissoba. I was nervous that day because it was the first time I visited a girlfriend's mother. I could not even talk straight... a rare thing in me!

The end of that relationship marked me most. I had the habit of going out with my friends and did not take her with me on those occasions. She hated that. One night, I called her from a phone booth. She said that I only had time for my friends and did not care about her and that was the reason she had cheated on me. That was April 1st. Of course with that, the relationship ended right at that moment. I still do not know whether she really cheated on me or said so to punish me. We never spoke to each other again.

The trio, fabulous friends for life

After Débora, the year of 2003 was dedicated to work. I was conscious of the need to finish my studies to get a better job, but chose to take double shifts for some more time to save money. In fact, I could not save as much as I thought I could. Another good thing happened for me in 2003. It was the formation of a trio of friends that lasts until today, even with the geographic distances that life imposes on us. Fábio, João Reis and I are this trio. For three years we constituted a fraternity, almost a family, united at all moments. There was only one thing spoiling our friendship and that was João Reis' love for a soccer team called Flamengo. I will tell how everything started.

One day, by chance, I met João Reis in the Ibirapuera Park. This place is similar to Battersea Park in London which some of you may know! Just like me, João used to walk in the park on Sundays, trying to find somebody he knew. There is a cafeteria where folks from Bahia normally met. When I saw him, I felt a great happiness. After all, we had not met in the last eight months. He had come to

São Paulo soon after we talked in Boninal and was now living with relatives in the south zone of the city. I still lived with my Aunt Nadir in the east side.

We talked a lot and found many things in common. We both worked downtown and wanted to live near the work places. We both wanted to break free from the loving imprisonment of our families, to have freedom to party. We knew that it was not going to be easy to pay the rent two ways only, so we decided to find a third fellow to share the expenses. I had already talked to Fábio about my intention to rent an apartment but, at the same time, I was aware of João Reis' antipathy towards him. So, I did not say anything just then. Anyway, Fábio wanted to abandon the tiny house where he lived with his sister and niece. I had to be very cautious over bringing the subject up with both of my friends. Finally, I very diplomatically suggested to João Reis to invite Fábio to share the apartment with us. In the beginning he resisted the idea, claiming that Fábio was a snob, but I was able to convince him that Fábio was a nice guy. We moved in together in the middle of the year. It was not easy to sign the contract because real estate agencies in São Paulo make extensive demands before accepting tenants. Everything worked out fine though, and there we were living in the center of São Paulo. I was the leader of the group because I was the only one with a regular job that had earnings and so able to sign the contract. I still worked as a cooperative valet at nights and during the days in a parking place right in front of our building. Fábio also worked near at the same pet shop and João Reis in a neighborhood close by that he could reach by foot. Perfect!

João Reis

Fábio

The first thing we did was talk to the janitor of the building, Mr Avelino, to make his acquaintance. He was a strong, bad-tempered man, but only before the first beer. Today, Mr Avelino is very fond of us. I took the key and went up the stairs carrying a mattress that I had bought nearby. What I wished the most, at that moment, was a good night's sleep. I had been working many hours a day, seven days a week in the last months, many times sleeping in the parking place.

In the following days, Fábio and João Reis also brought their stuff. At the beginning it was weird to see them together. João Reis is a very bad tempered man. Fábio, by turn, is slothful and always ready to make a joke out of any situation. For a short period I was the go-between and the one who maintained the peace. Fortunately, things worked out fine. When they both finally understood each other they turned into great friends. In fact, João Reis was Fábio's best man when he married Fernanda, a girl he met in that very building. Fábio and Fernanda are now parents to Anna Júlia.

As in any friendship, some misunderstandings and disagreements came up, but we overcame them quickly. I learned more and more in those times of conviviality. Here is a list of what I have learned with my fellows: with João Reis, to be stronger and more determined; with Fábio, my love for fashion and an ability to cook. Living in that apartment, I discovered many of my own shortcomings. My friends showed me that some of my habits were not healthy. Our trio had its athletic moments too. There is a viaduct, nicknamed Big Worm, which is closed to cars on weekends. There we jogged every Sunday morning. In the afternoons, we played soccer. Nowadays, I organize soccer matches on-board the cruise ships where I work.

Our friendship is excellent. My fellows and I formed a friendship that became a legend in the neighborhood. I believe that the only person that does not miss us is Mr Avelino, the janitor. I keep from explaining why, because it is not flattering for us!

Friends for life

vimeo.com/114745689

Adventures in the neighborhood

The best memories of those three years living together as a trio were the birthday parties. The best one only ended when the cops came by.

I switched jobs again, but always keeping double shifts. My main job was the work in the cooperative. I was skinny, working that much. My credit card account, however, did not stay slim! In order to obtain labor compensation I asked the car parking company to dismiss me. I took that dismissal money and bought—guess what?— a Honda motorbike!

The cooperative administrator assigned me to serve as the valet parker in a fancy hairdresser salon in a rich neighborhood where I met many interesting people.

My 25th birthday

One of them was Fe, a girl who would become my girlfriend and with whom I had a tragic bike accident. I will write about this later. What I want to tell now is about the women I knew at the salon. We three amigos were single and gave private parties in our apartment. On a Sunday, August 10th, 2003, two days after my birthday, we filled the apartment with friends including all the women who worked in the salon. I invited neighbors and people I knew in the building's vicinity. By that time I had a cell phone and called everybody I knew. I had asked for Mr Avelino's permission, assuring him that the party was meant only for a few friends. I could not have imagined the numbers of people who accepted the invitation. Friends invited friends who invited more friends. People from the salon brought some bottles of sake, the Japanese wine made from rice. My co-worker from the parking place, Cowboy, brought with him some bottles of vodka. I bought sixteen packs of beer. Since we lived in the top floor we had planned a barbecue. There were over 60 people in our apartment.

In the beginning everybody behaved. Then the drinks were served and all good conduct disappeared. Less than two hours later the party was unbearable. Mr Avelino showed up at the door, looking for who was responsible for the mess! He told us to keep the noise down because the neighbors were complaining. As he spoke we were silent. But as he turned his back the chaos began again. The worst thing, however, was yet to come. My friend Cowboy found himself a girl and, seeing no space inside the apartment, he took her to the stairway to cuddle in privacy. Unfortunately this was right in front of Mr Avelino's apartment. The janitor reprimanded him harshly, he retaliated, and so Mr Avelino ended up calling the police. The cops came and put an end to our party. The next day, I received a warning and a fine!

More troubles

The year 2003 was not yet ended and João Reis and I prepared to drive the Honda to the São Paulo seashore. After an entire day at a barbecue with the company he worked for, he was almost asleep on the back of my motorbike. I was driving irresponsibly, I admit it, and we were nearly in an accident. With the shock, João Reis fully awoke. This near miss never vanished from my mind. Today I think that I gained a new life that night. Maybe it was God's warning. I do not know. What I know is that, sometime later, I would receive another warning.

But one story at a time!

We arrived at the shore safe and sound. After saying hello to the fellows in the house we rented we went to the beach. João Reis stayed by the bike, taking care of it, and I went for a walk. The beach was crowded, many people offered champagne to celebrate New Year's Eve. That was my last memory. I woke up at home with a terrible hangover and João Reis yelling at me. He shouted that I should have let him know that I was going home in Robério's car. How could I? I could remember nothing…as you can see, I drank too much and too irresponsibly. What happened should have made me aware of an omen of a tragedy. I did not pay attention. Five months later I would learn a big lesson.

Upside down

Working at the beauty salon I met many people, as I said. Fe was a slender, smiley person and was the most special of them to me. She lived in the same neighborhood where Débora lived but I did not care about that. At first we only exchanged glances. The salon environment was very professional and we treated each other professionally too. One day a friend of mine let me know that Fe was interested in me. I could not believe it. Me? I was not yet really recovered from that sad time with my Japanese passion.

All the salon workers used to go dancing, on Friday nights. That Friday though, was special because it was the 14th of May and Fe's 22nd birthday. The group was cheerful. At the dance place, after enough beers to inebriate an entire regiment of soldiers, the same friend whispered in my ear that Fe was telling everyone that I was the only birthday present she wanted. Well, I think that is not polite to say no to a woman... I leave the rest of what happened at the dance for the reader to imagine.

The bar closed early, before midnight. In the neighborhood, there was no other affordable place to go on celebrating. Somebody remembered a bar some miles away, by the interstate highway and we decided to go there. I offered Fe a ride on my Honda. She did not want to accept because her brother, as a motorcycle courier, had suffered quite a few accidents and her mother would not let her ride on a bike. She accepted, in the end, and we all went to the bar, with the rest of the group following in two cars. The price of beer was fair, and we drank a lot. Around three o'clock in the morning, I was feeling like a super hero and told Fe that I would drive her home. She asked if I was sober enough to drive. I answered that I was fine, that I was a hell of a driver and that I knew the city like my own backyard. Of course, nobody in the group was sober, and me least of all. I could not admit I was drunk to the woman I had just won.

We left the bar on that cold dawn of Saturday, May 15th, 2004. It was my first time on that side of the town. I did not know the place so I followed the traffic signs. I crossed one street at a speed of about 40 miles per hour. With no time for thinking or deviating, I violently crashed my bike against the front of a black Citröen. With the impact, I flew off. For a few seconds I was very confused. I was wearing a helmet and did not suffer anything to my head, but my right foot was hurt—I had hit the headlight and lost a shoe. Fe was lying on the ground, crying, shouting my name, desperate. I panicked. The couple in the Citröen called the ambulance and told me to stay on the ground where I was and to not move. I did not follow their advice—I had to see if Fe was OK. I could not do anything to help her fractured leg and we had to wait for the paramedics. In the meantime the Citröen driver told me that I was driving the wrong way. I had not seen the sign and drove down the street in the wrong direction. I only thought of Fe's mother warning her not to ride a motorbike.

The paramedics took us to hospital. They told me to leave the bike at the accident spot because the police needed to make a report. Miraculously the effect of alcohol was suddenly gone. The physician examined us and after a while we were released. In my opinion he made a mistake because Fe was having a hypoglycemic attack. There was also the issue of her fractured leg that needed attention!

At this point I learned that it is better to have friends than money. João Reis arrived to the police station thirty minutes after I called him. Fábio, who was at his girlfriend's house, arrived almost at the same time. The chief police officer was kind enough to release us and we rescued the bike. But later we had to take Fe to the hospital again because she fainted. João Reis drove an old Chevette at that time—there is always a Chevette in my life—so he took us. The doctor medicated her and thankfully she got better. I cannot go on without saying that João Reis has always showed he is a true friend.

Before we got to Fe's house, she used João Reis' cell phone to call her brother, asking him to prepare her mother for what happened. I handed her over to her brother's arms because she could not walk alone. Her fractured leg, in fact, got much worse, preventing her from working for six months. All that time she was in bed I felt really cut-up inside. It was the worst period of my life. Sharing these memories in this book makes me feel a little better, a little at peace.

In the days after the accident, I visited her, with a broken heart. I suffered, because I knew the damage I caused to the entire family. There was another factor that contributed to my heartache: Fe was a mother to a three-year-old girl. I would later find out that she had once been married for two years.

Lesson

As I said, I visited Fe with a sad heart. We had kissed each other the night before, but what should I say to her now? What did she really mean to me? A one-night stand, that was all. Nevertheless, I would carry the world on my shoulders, because I put her in that situation. I should admit my mistake and face the problem. When I entered the room I gave her a book and kissed her. Our relationship began at that very moment. After that kiss our lives changed.

So far I had been living the life of a single man, with two other single friends and we had no concern of what tomorrow would bring. But from that day on I started a new life. Seeing Fe, young and healthy and clever, with a beautiful child, lying in that bed without being able to walk, made me think about what I had done. I was the only one to blame. My family raised me to think that causing evil to anyone is a sin, and as such, this situation tortured me. I lived dog's days. I visited her almost every day. We became good friends, and finally girlfriend and boyfriend. She ended up falling in love with me but I did not feel the same though. The thing is that I pitied her.

After six months of agony Fe was more in love and I had kept the relationship going because of my guilt. In an attempt to compensate her, I took her to physiotherapy sessions, gave her books and chocolates. I was bound to her and her family but even so I knew that I did not love her. As she recovered I tried to have a normal life. I started reading self-help books. She finally recovered, thank God. For me, what remained was a great lesson. I still drink my beers, but I am much more responsible now. By the way, after the accident, I sold my Honda motorbike. Nowadays drinking and driving make no sense to me. I do not have a car, although I can afford one. I prefer to not take risks like the one I just told you, because the next might have a dreadful conclusion.

Breaking up with Fe was painful, for her and for me. However, it was necessary. I resumed my routine. After reading so many self-help books, I found out that I knew very little about life.

By the end of 2004, after so much suffering, I would take the largest step of my life and I went back to school. I wanted to leave the blindness I had been in for so long. Previously, I thought that only by switching jobs I would be happier. One event helped me with my decision. This time, the job abandoned me. The hair beauty salon closed down and as the cooperative administrator I was assigned elsewhere and now worked from seven to seven. I am proud to say that the cooperative maintained a high school course sponsored by the Brazilian Industry Service, with classes twice a week. In January 2005, I enrolled in the course.

Back to school

The classes started at 7:30pm. The teachers, Magda and Nicoleta, were very good and helped me very much. As I always make lots of noise with everything I do, I convinced João Reis, even with his high school diploma, to join me. After completing the course, I tried to enter a state university, but I did not succeed. Alessandro and his wife Tatiana also began to take classes there. Alessandro had already got a profession as a dog clipper, but he knew about the importance of study. We were together for some time in school, but he dropped the course, and so did João Reis. They had other priorities. I remained in the classes, like an orphan. I was determined, however, to finish high school. My teachers said that, depending on my efforts, I could get the diploma in less than a year. But after the midterm exams, I realized that the rhythm was too slow for me. I decided to look for another school with classes every day, so I could accelerate my course. I found one, very convenient because I could get there by foot from the place I worked. In fact, I had to walk because there was no bus service between the two places.

I finished work by 7:00pm and my classes started at 7:30, so I had to rush, without a shower or dinner. I lived on mortadella sandwiches that I ate at the parking place. But I was hungry for something else: knowledge. I studied seriously. I visited several libraries in the city, looking for books that could broaden my horizon. I spent many nights watching educational videos in a video player Alessandro had lent to me. I took many examinations and finally completed the course.

When we study, doors open to us. Our mind opens as well. It was no different for me. I heard many encouraging words from my teachers, one of them in particular. Carlos, my Chemistry teacher, told me to pursue my dreams. The phrase fitted like a glove to me; I had been lost but found my way by leaving the blindness of ignorance.

I decided to go to the Renaissance Hotel once more. I had only two exams to take, Chemistry and Physics, to conclude the course and achieve the diploma. I passed in front of the hotel every day. One day I stopped by to once again fill-in an application form. Now I had all they demanded from me: three years experience as a parking valet, a regular driver's license and the high school course completed.

I repeated what I had done before. I arrived early, stood in line with the first fifty candidates and filled-in the form. When they called me for interview, I realized that the girl was not the same. I felt the adrenaline, and was surer of myself. When the girl asked me about high school, I said to myself, "those who speak the truth shall not be punished", and explained that I still had two exams before receiving the diploma. She nodded, said that she understood, but explained that I needed to have the diploma before applying for the job.

Once again, I left the hotel, sad and disappointed. Looking back, though, the year was good for me. I had found a person that would help very much in my determination to win. But this is a subject for the next chapter.

The first time I met Marcela (center)

Chapter 9

Loving is evolving

In 2005 I met Marcela Gonçalves, born in Bahia state like me. She had long black hair, a beautiful face and a slim majestic body. She was intelligent, determined and adorable!

Let me tell you how we met and what the importance of this woman was as she fondly helped me in the rise of my career. I hope to be able to write sufficiently well to do justice to Marcela.

The first time I saw that gorgeous woman was in May in a post-Carnival party at the university in São Paulo. It was a warm sunny Sunday. I had met, some time before, one guy named Manoel Alves who was also from Bahia and a car valet like me. He was 26 years old, short, bald, blue-eyed, smiley and incredibly optimistic. Today he is married to Shirley and they have their little Geovana. I will tell you more later about him. Now it is important to mention him because he was the Cupid for Marcela and me. My first impression of him was not so good because by being a shorty and bald he had the appearance of a bad-tempered man. He also sounded arrogant by way of an attitude since he had worked at the company longer than me. The first impression proved untrue and we became good friends. It was his idea to go to the party. He in fact insisted on me going with him. His final attempt at persuasion was decisive; he wished to introduce me to a lovely friend of his!

Marcela and Manoel had been childhood friends in Bahia. Lately they had not seen each other often but kept in contact through the Internet. Incredible as it might sound, this is a resource I was not really aware of at that time! Manoel told Marcela to meet us at the party. He warned me, however, to keep my distance from her because she was a family girl and he knew my bad reputation. It seemed to me that he was definitely jealous and protective as he talked about her with great tenderness.

We arrived at the party full of expectations. I confess that I was more interested in the party than in Marcela. It was exciting to be among the university students. I paid the astonishing price of US$30 for a t-shirt. This was set as the price to get into the party.

When Manoel introduced me to Marcela her beauty immediately impressed me. So much that I had no courage to make, let us say, a romantic approach. The environment was chic, the event grandiose and the girl nothing less than gorgeous. Marcela studied Law at the time. She was too good for me I thought. We talked much about our place of origin, the friends we missed and all those things that people talk about when they are far from home. Between us, however, a coincidence existed that only God could explain. Although she lived in a town 240 miles away from Boninal, we found a friend in common. This friend was Shirley who today is Manoel's wife! Shirley did not go to the party that day because she was working in a shopping center store, as she usually did on a Sunday. Shirley and I had not talked for quite some time and she would never imagine what destiny was preparing for her. Our lives would change from that day on.

It was now Manoel's turn to get curious. He never stopped asking questions about Shirley. So that was how things happened: I became a friend of Manoel's friend and he wanted to become a friend of my friend who was also a friend of his friend. Puzzling perhaps?

The party ended, and we left very happy, with a nice sensation that a good friendship had begun. By way of a payback, the next day Manoel insisted on me giving him Shirley's telephone number. I said that I could not give it to him because of his bad reputation and the fact that Shirley was a family girl.

He insisted, so finally I asked Marcela to make contact with Shirley to ask her permission to give her number to Manoel. She said yes, they talked, set a date and instantaneously fell in love with each other. In less than two months they were living together. Nowadays they are married and live in Bahia. Shirley is a schoolteacher and Manoel is a salesperson. Their daughter Geovana is Marcela's god-daughter.

Marcela and I went out for a first date. Then we went out again and then one more time. We officially got together in July 2005. I was enamored. Moreover, I was very proud for dating a Law student and I told all my friends. We were together for over a year and I learned and matured very much in that period. Attending the high school, I dreamed of a graduation in Tourism. I admit that this was mainly to become intellectually closer to Marcela who I saw as someone so much better than I was. I did not mean to compare, but I felt for Marcela the same admiration I felt for Débora.

My relationship with Marcela gave me a different awareness of myself through a range of sensations. At times I was very happy for being with the woman I loved. At other times I was surprised by my very low self-esteem, thinking that I did not deserve to be her boyfriend.

We had many happy moments, together. There was a special one, which especially marked me because I learned an important lesson. I will explain. Marcela was a very strict girl and was aware of her rights as a citizen; maybe that was the reason why she attended Law School. One day Manoel bought

Marcela (left) and Shirley

four tickets for a party; he informed the cashier that we were students but did not get the 50% discount. Marcela, at the time was working as an apprentice in a Law firm. She made contact with the event organization, presented our students IDs and demanded to have the discount. I did not believe we could beat those giants, but they understood that Marcela was not kidding. The manager invited her to his office, where nobody could see what was going on, and delivered the four t-shirts for half of the price. You can imagine how proud I was of my girlfriend. It was a good beginning for Marcela who today is a well-established lawyer in São Paulo. That was how she taught me to fight for my rights. Later on, I successfully appealed twice to the Brazilian Department of Consumer Protection and Defense. Marcela and I were no longer together but I had learned my lesson. She taught me some other things, for example, to value family. It was very good to see her behavior towards her father and mother. Her attitude led me to feel guilty because sometimes I hardly called my mom. Nowadays, even when I am abroad, I call my mom every other day. I realize exactly how important my mother is for me and how much she fought to give me a dignified life. Marcela was the one who taught me to recognize that.

I admit the mistakes I made during my relationship with Marcela. I guess I have this difficulty, like my father, to make relationships last. She broke up with me and I went through some bad times after her decision. I was losing the perfect companion and the woman with whom I had planned to have children. Even though I was 27 years old then I was not ready to get married. I knew, as she did, that maintaining the relationship would not be good for either of us. Marcela was methodical. She never abandoned her plans to finish studies and graduate. Some time after we broke up she was moving back to Bahia to work at an important law firm. I actually hoped that we could be together again and was devastated. She had already put a sentimental distance between us and now there was a geographic distance keeping us apart. I mourned my loss for quite a while. I could not sleep. I lost weight.

Fortunately I found somebody with the gift of the word to support me or reprimand me when necessary. This someone was my cousin Ednalva. She is a nice and clever woman. She counseled me to read and to look for God. Although we lived in different states, we talked every day. In my distress I spent lots of my money on telephone calls to her. Ednalva gave me the idea for this book. She believed that writing could be a way for me to overcome my grief. I could not do it, at least not at that moment. I was desperate. I did not accept the end of the relationship. It was a hard time, almost as hard as the angst

I went through after the accident with my motorbike. It seemed to me that I was the one in bed this time, unable to walk. I was down and out, with no self-esteem at all. I cried. I cried to my friends Robério and Alessandro. Only in front of João Reis I refrained from crying because for him it was unacceptable for a man to cry for a woman.

For months, I wept and I felt angry. Thanks to my friends I got over it. I began to see how much I had learned during my time with Marcela and finally I admitted that she was not the one to blame. And so I changed my mind. I thought my happiness was in her hands but now I know my happiness depends on me and rests in my own hands.

In order to escape from my agony I started an English course in the Brazilian Service of Commerce. Without knowing, Marcela was once again helping me. There is a saying that goes like this: "Some people help us when they enter our lives, and help us even more after they leave."

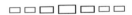

Chapter 10

Breaking stones and dividing waters

By the end of 2005 I reached one of my main achievements in São Paulo. Without ceremony, alone on a cold Wednesday night, I received my high school degree.

I failed to seize the opportunity of achieving this in Bahia even with all the facilities: school close to my house, uniform, books, family and friends' support. In São Paulo, in order to obtain my diploma, I faced all the obstacles, and that is why I value so much this conquest. Maybe this does not mean so much for many people, but for me it was like receiving a passport.

The first thing I did was to enroll in the College of Tourism. I badly wanted to go to university. The first reason was that I would be entitled to apply for a job at the Hotel Renaissance, which had been one of my main objectives for a long time. Another reason was that I considered it beautiful to hear people saying that they had attended a graduation course. In fact, I still think so.

As a tourism expert, I would spend my life traveling all over the world, performing a duty that I love, making money and having a good time. That was my idea of a dream job. I admit that this is the naivety of someone just starting their academic life. Now I know exactly what a tourism expert does. And now I have a dream job.

Starting a new life

In January 2006 I passed in the selection process for the college. I was counting on the promise of a 50% scholarship by means of the car valets union. I felt like a new life was starting for me. In the beginning of February, I went to the registrar's office to make my enrollment. The excitement did not last long though. The governmental office did not issue my certificate in time. I explained that it was not my fault, but the college was inflexible and I could not enroll. You can imagine my disappointment. I had just lost one entire year of my life because of bureaucracy! Anyway, I could not retreat. I knew that it was important to know languages and I looked for a course to learn Spanish. Since I was a boy, I used to read some of my sister's handbooks in that language and found it interesting how close it is to Portuguese. I hated the English language, maybe because of a nasty teacher I had, back in Boninal. During high school I did not have to worry because English was not a mandatory subject in the curriculum. If it had been, I most certainly would have failed it. Nevertheless, I also knew that a tourism expert must be fluent in English. Therefore, I had to study English. For some time, to delay my search, I used the excuse that I had not enough money to pay for the course.

Then again, I remembered Marcela had suggested that I apply for a scholarship to the Brazilian Service of Commerce at Senac. Although I lived only three blocks away from the Senac building, I had never gone there. I used to look at the building as a distant unreachable dream. I was poor, how could I ever study with those people I saw there... perfumed, well dressed, and looking wealthy?

Anyway, I was determined. Embarrassed to go there in person, I used a phone booth in the street to ask about my chances of acceptance in the course. The woman was very polite on the phone. The Senac team is very good at providing assistance. She informed me that I could apply for what they call the social responsibility scholarship but that I would not be able to get approval in time to attend the upcoming course programmed for February 9th. Again, not very exciting news! This meant that I would have to pay US$600 for the semester to do the Basic One course, an amount that represented a fortune for me at that time. I decided to enroll anyhow, since they allowed me to pay in five installments. That way I could do this course while I waited for the scholarship to continue with the next modules. If I could get the scholarship, everything would work in my favor.

I had the vivid sensation of being parachuted directly into the English class. Already tense, I was tired after a 12-hour shift in the parking place, I held the course book. The teacher came in and said "good evening, how are you?" and I almost ran out to the street. I could not understand a single word. "Good night" was the only expression I was familiar with. The teacher was very helpful in beginning that way. He noticed I was hesitant to talk and said a few words for me in Portuguese. He asked us to talk about ourselves, name, profession and the reason why we were studying English.

Learning English

vimeo.com/114745690

Facing challenges

I was the only person in the class without a college degree. I kept looking at these thirteen people in the classroom, all well dressed and confident. I was neither well dressed nor confident! I remember each one of them: the accountant Donizete; the tourism expert Fernando Neves; the administrators Fabíola and André; an engineer that claimed to have built the Higienopolis Shopping Center (God almighty!); a nutritionist; and my friend Erone Feitosa, a designer, who helped me with this book. I saw everyone and I felt intimidated, because they already had some knowledge of the English language. They knew the names of their professions. I was in shock. When it was my turn, everyone turned their head in my direction. I tried my best and managed to say something. The teacher was pleased and proceeded with the class. During the break between classes, I talked to the others and found that they all had taken English classes before! So my mind had made more of it than was the actual situation. I have learnt to be wary of this as it makes life far tougher than it need be.

The next class was also a torment. I was like a fat person in his first day at the gym, surrounded by men and women in excellent shape, all working out. I was worried that my colleagues thought "What is this guy doing here? He has not a minimal chance to learn anything…" I persisted day after day, every Tuesday and Thursday, I wanted to go home and never again set foot in Senac.

It was a tense time spending hours with those people whom I considered far better than I was.

There was a man in the group. He made me the target of his jokes. I took my mobile phone to the classroom just once. The phone rang and it was important to answer it. The man made acid remarks in English about my behavior. He always found opportunities to diminish me before our colleagues, showing off his knowledge of English. For instance, when he saw me entering the class he used to say, "The drugs have arrived". When I finally understood the meaning of the expression I felt really hurt. He was thinking of me as a drug dealer. I come from a family that loathes illicit drugs. In classes I began to lose confidence and concentration.

When the final exams were approaching I feared I would fail and lose the scholarship I needed so much. I could not afford another module. Besides, my credit was still restricted because of the damned credit card. However, I survived the first module of the course thanks to my teacher Marcos. He talked to me and what he said made me respect him forever. "Martin, I can see that you have difficulties, but I also see your willpower and dedication. Do not worry about people who make fun of you; most of them already know some English and I know you don't, but do not think that they know it all. They may think they do, or pretend they do. Nevertheless, you and they are here in Basic One. Listen, what you have to do is study twice as much as they do. While they drink on the weekends you should be studying. When you feel tired, study a little more. At the end, you will see the result." Those words entered my head like a chip in a mobile phone.

I was not sure of getting a scholarship for Basic Two, because my grade was low, but I applied following the advice of the woman who first helped me on the phone. Some days later, they called me for an interview with a social worker. I was nervous about the information, and then I relaxed. If I needed to state that I had no money to go on studying I would not be lying.

Exactly on time, I was there for the interview wearing my work uniform. It would be a way to exhibit myself as a low-paid worker. You know, a picture is worth a thousand words. Besides, my appearance helped as I did look like a poor fellow. On my way to the interview, I made God a promise… if I got that scholarship, I would dedicate myself to study as never before.

A very polite social worker, Cleidimara Coral Perla, interviewed me. She had that gift, it seemed, of reading my mind while I spoke. And I spoke the truth, telling her that I really wanted to study. At the end of the interview she asked who had paid for the module Basic One. I told her that I had, through hard work and dedication, working 12 hour shifts at my car parking attendant job. I said that almost crying. I guess it may have worked. Anyway, she left the room without giving me an answer. I left too, very confident. After all, I was just a poor guy looking for a place under the sun.

Helping hands

By Thursday, just a few hours before the beginning of Basic Two, a sweet voice called me on the phone. Judging by the voice, the girl would be marvelous. She said she was a Senac's clerk and was calling to let me know that I had been given a 100% scholarship. Those words were poetry to my ears. I started jumping like crazy, a 26 years old big baby. My colleagues did not understand anything and even though I explained, they did not know how important it was to get a scholarship. Who cares about what they think? I was dreaming about the new world that knowledge would show me. I realized that, along with the scholarship, came the responsibility of being an exemplary student. I decided that my minimum grade should be a B. How would I get such a high grade? With help!

Another teacher offered me the help I needed. This time it was Emiliano, a nice fellow from the south, with blond hair. He became an essential part of my success during my course. I was eager to learn and he had a passion for teaching. I felt like a philosopher's apprentice, asking for the "whys" of life.

By then, I was not the sheepish student I had been before. My attitude changed and I showed discipline and courage. Teacher Emiliano helped me to see the world differently. He asked us to listen to a CD and so I did. I heard it five, eight, eleven times if I needed to so that I could catch on. He oriented me to go back to the Basic One books, available at the library. I took four books, the maximum quantity allowed, and two days later I went back to take four more. He recommended that we write. I wrote so much that several times we stayed after classes to discuss my errors. One time he had to run off to punch his time card and then came back to continue correcting my writing. He also enjoyed playing the guitar for the students. I began to listen to music and I watched movies as I never had before. I lived intensely at that time and today, I continue to do so.

Everything seemed so interesting and so enchanting in relation to English speaking countries. Political organization, financial systems, schools and public transportation, every little thing was important to me. With another group of thirteen students I learned so much. In spite of the discrimination, harassing and intimidation I learned. For them, I was just the "little Bahian" of the group. They did not care that I am very proud of being a Bahian. Thirteen people. Maybe because of my classroom colleagues, the number 13 came to be my lucky number.

I evolved. I was not an ignorant person anymore. Now my colleagues and me took part in class conversations. A colleague asked to borrow my school notebook. Was the secret of my evolution in the notes? She was disappointed, because I had no more than three written pages. Everything I knew was stored in my cerebral chip.

During the World Soccer Cup of 2006 in Germany, I watched the matches on TV. Today I have not as much enthusiasm for soccer. Anyway, that competition, even having Brazil defeated by France, ended in a positive way for me. It may sound silly, but there was a magic moment for me. A reporter asked the coach of the Brazilian national soccer team, Carlos Alberto Parreira, to say something in English about his technical scheme. I knew a lot about soccer at that time and was very pleased to realize that I understood what he said. It had all been spoken in good and plain English. This impressed me so much that I was very encouraged and decided after that to study even more.

Friends

In Senac I made two real friends. Ana Paula joined the course in the beginning of Basic

Erone

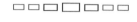

Two. Erone became my friend a little later. From Ana Paula I received much more than I could ever give in return, an enormous amount of support. She noticed my difficulty but not once discriminated against me. On the contrary, she shared with me what she had learned in other courses she attended. She deserves admiration. Every time I am in Brazil I visit her and her husband Ricardo.

I will talk about these two friends in the next chapter.

□ □ □ ☐ □ □ □

Ana

Chapter 11

A friend is one who cheers us up

I reserved this chapter for two friends. These are two special people that accepted me as I was, never imposing old prejudicial regional barriers that still persist in some places. Erone Feitosa and Ana Paula are these two women.

I started the course like a child on their first day of school. Frightened, observing everything and ready to leave even before the class began. I was feeling like an Indian of a distant tribe in the white man's space. How could I ever learn such a difficult language? I sought refuge in each look and found no warmth. But then I did. There were friendly looks in my direction but, even so, I was still scared and afraid that I could not do anything right. I realized these two girls were there for me. Now I realize that the emotional distance and sense of disconnection was the natural rhythm of a city. I was not in Boninal anymore, a place where everybody knows everybody and there were no strangers. Now strangers were to become friends. Finally, we got to know each other and made true friendships. I guess they represented the opening of doors to me on that course.

I could talk endlessly about all the support I had from Erone and Ana Paula, but this space is too short. If I ever write my full autobiography, there will be a chapter dedicated to both of them. In my heart, they already occupy a large space.

Senac success ... a milestone achieved ... a stepping stone laid

I finished the tenth and final module of the Senac English course in April 2009. I was the only student to finish the course. My average grade was A minus and I had the honor of being an exemplary scholar, fulfilling all my duties.

Organizations like Senac always look to the future. I adopted this approach as a way to live my life. Thanks to Senac I gained a scholarship that has brought me professional work and rewards that I could never have imagined. Because I learnt English, I found new jobs and could make money. Sometime later, I went back to Senac and took other courses, such as computer technology and bar management—this time happily paying for the classes. These courses further improved my chances to work away in other parts of the world.

In Senac's classrooms, I met wonderful people. I made friends with many of them and keep in touch today. And I cannot forget my teachers Marcos, Emiliano, Juliana Cavaliere and Pedrina Godofredo. My two special friends wrote me some lines that I would like to share ...

My friend, the winner by Erone Feitosa

When I first saw you, in our Senac classroom, I was surprised that you knew nothing of English, because it is usual for all students to have some contact with the language in junior high. Anyway, it made no difference to me, because the Basic One course is designed for people who want to start from zero.

Then, some people made fun of you, but you made considerable efforts, instead of giving up: took your compositions to the teachers to correct, asked which books to read and studied harder and harder. You managed to pass Basic One. After that, you obtained the best grades.

I noticed that, the more your English improved, the more self-assured you became. Including the decision of switching jobs. When the hotel Renaissance hired you, we met a couple of times in that beautiful building, to have dinner or go to the theater. By then, you had straight shoulders, a confident glance, knew how to be sympathetic and were often talkative. I always liked the way you think. You set goals to reach. Since the beginning you reached them all.

I was very happy to see your pictures from your work in the United States on your first contract abroad. Then you sent me another picture, showing you in front of the Tower of Pisa. After, that, another one in a Formula 1 race car, in Monaco. You sent me many more pictures, afterwards. I realized that you had become a citizen of the world and a new man.

Now I know that you travel around the world, with firm steps. Your will power and determination are the weapons you use to fight prejudice.

I am always happy to have you near me.

Erone

My friend, the citizen of the world

Today, Martin visited me in my house. After a long while without seeing each other, it was great to remember old stories and tell new ones. Martin has a super way about him. My friend at the English course has changed quite a bit. Now he has rich experience, not only as a professional but also as a man. The Boninal boy is now a citizen of the world, a most traveled person, a businessman, a writer, sharing everything he has experienced on his journey.

Martin is always busy, one moment he is in São Paulo, the next moment he is showing Brazil to some friend he made on his travels a board the ships he has worked on. In spite of all these commitments, he always finds the time to accomplish everything he plans. He makes things happen, forever smiling. He is a good person.

He turned his life into a trip, relishing every single moment, simplifying things that everybody seems to complicate. He does not show off; instead, he simply lives the good, simple, true things that life presents to us.

It is not possible to compare the old, hesitant Martin I met years ago with this man that I see today: self-assured, matured, filled with a variety of experiences. I remember the past, situations we faced in the Senac English course. One day I told him about how impressed I was with his quick evolution, and asked what he was doing to learn so fast. He said, "Ana, I take every opportunity in my day, at home or at work, to study: I do my homework twice or three times. I repeat the lessons." Then I said, "Martin, the result is great, because you really are getting better every day." Then he surprised me again, by saying that a colleague refused his company, in the first module of the course. He said that with sadness in his voice and I could see how hurt he was by the rejection. Most certainly, this experience made him study harder, to overcome all obstacles. At that exact moment, I could feel that he would go very far. Not many people face their fears with such courage. Martin has.

Martin was always cheerful in the classes, joking and making us smile. If he had not told me, I would never guess that he felt uncomfortable by being the poorest person in the class.

He kept the ball rolling at all times. He never blamed life or destiny. He just focused on his objectives and overcame limitations. His experience is proof that determination and hard work make us get wherever we want to go. Martin shows us, all the time, that cheerfulness makes the daily battle very much easier to fight.

Ana Paula

Ana Paula's video tribute

vimeo.com/115608534

Chapter 12

One step from heaven

Once more, I tried my luck at the Renaissance Hotel. It was my third attempt at the end of 2006 but I now felt a lot more confident. I was working as the person in charge of 15 car valets and my wage was twice as much as the salary the hotel paid for its valets. Anyhow, to work there had become an obsession for me. Therefore, I went.

I had just participated in a four-day immersion course, speaking only in English. To be prepared for the interview and meeting, I had carefully studied the hotel website.

Following the routine that I was already so aware of, I filled in the form and waited for the interview. I was expecting to hear a question about my skills in English. The question came up, and I was more than pleased to inform the lady that I could speak English, if required. She said that it was not necessary. I was disappointed. Again I left the hotel without an answer. A few days later, I received a call. Selma, one of the hotel desk clerks, with very polite manners, said that I had passed the first phase of selection and that I should talk to the hotel parking place manager, David Riboldi. She suggested a date for the interview and of course I immediately accepted this.

By the end of November of 2006, there I was again. By now I felt as if I was almost a hotel customer! I entered the Human Resources department of the hotel, as nervous as I had been the first time. There, beautiful and well-educated women spoke on the phone. One of them offered me a cup of coffee that I politely declined. I was afraid that the coffee would make me more anxious than I already was. Not long after that, an elegantly dressed man called my name. In his office, the first question he asked me was my reason for accepting a job for half the wage I was earning. I explained that my experience working in the cooperative at the hotel garage had been such a wonderful time and that the hotel impressed me. I explained that the hotel benefits would compensate the difference in my salary. I spoke about their internal promotion scheme, the benefits the employees were entitled to; I showed him that I knew the hotel's routine and finally I stated that nothing would prevent me from working at the hotel. He appeared to be satisfied with what he heard, explaining that he was going to interview some more candidates for the three vacancies and that I would get an answer by phone. In fact, I had an answer only a few days later.

I carried my mobile phone in my pocket all the time, afraid of missing the call. I remember exactly where I was when the phone rang. I will never forget that moment. The same nice voice, Selma, told me that I was the new valet parker of the Renaissance São Paulo Hotel. I started the job on December 4th, 2006. The call restored my self-esteem. Actually, it changed my life forever. The Renaissance Hotel was, for me, everything I thought it would be, and

A long way from my life in Boninal

I fell in love with the place. To begin with, we were "forced" to follow a three-day training called "In the Beginning". It was a great training course—our first and only duties involved eating, drinking and sleeping for one night in a suite so that we could experience being a guest. In order to offer a service of excellence the company's vision was for all employees to have an idea of how the guests should feel. One other "task" was to order room service. Can you believe this? I had to eat five-star food, for free, to know how guests would feel about the hotel and its services.

Seriously, it was a party. I loved each day of the training. Not long before, I had taken a lunch-box to work; now, I was having breakfast and lunch with the gringos. Unimaginable! Unfortunately, the training was soon over but I did participate in other training courses. I paid attention to every piece of information to learn all I know in terms of good service. Those who have ever worked at that hotel are proud to tell everybody about it. As I do.

Life was not easy at the garage, however. But I was amused with everything. People did not understand why I could be so happy, being a simple valet parker—I heard that quite a lot. The answer was simple: I drove all day long and I love to drive and I was proud to be a hotel employee after so many trials. Actually, I thanked God everyday and performed my duties as well as I could. In the meantime I worked for better days to come. Indeed they came. I did all I could to be helpful to every foreign guest because I wanted to interact with them and practice English. Many times, when they needed assistance to call a taxi or get information about directions, I insisted on helping them. I was the only valet parker that could speak English so I had an advantage over the others. One guest, an American fellow, is today a good friend of mine.

The language of love

It happens everywhere. When a man gets involved with a woman, it is always good to have another man to talk to. One day this American friend, at that time a guest of the hotel, asked me to help him. He had met a beautiful Brazilian girl but she did not speak English. As always, I was ready to help and found it all very amusing. I assumed the position of interpreter for both of them. For me, that was not simply practicing English, but it was an intensive course of how foreigners behave with girls. I learned some guerrilla love tactics that I use when I am abroad. I did the job without receiving a single dollar, but with great pleasure. My friendship with this American started that day. We even went out together, we three, for dinner. Later, every time he came to Brazil, he had a new girlfriend and, several times, I served again as interpreter. This type of inclusion is not usual when working in hospitality.

Nice fellow

I have many funny stories to tell about the three years I worked at the hotel.

However, there is something serious to talk about. I have to write a few words about David Riboldi, my supervisor for almost a year at the hotel and also my friend. He was a sensible person, who spoke the language of employees, making simple the complicated tasks of his department. I told him two days before writing this paragraph that I have never found a boss so friendly and to be such a jolly good fellow as he was. He did not even know about this book. He helped me in many ways, from my beginning there until the two promotions I achieved. Being completely honest, he was great behind the scenes. When we talked, I remembered two people that I suggested for work at the hotel: Jesus, who left a little while ago, and Flávio, a nice person who is still working with David.

One time, when I was the valet parker, David appointed me employee of the month for good performance. The hotel was like a small town with 450 inhabitants and I got along with people in all departments. Soon I started receiving offers for other departments. One of the call center supervisors invited me to work with him. But I was afraid of speaking in English on the phone, so I declined the offer. The closest I got to a promotion was in security; Eduardo, a supervisor, told me that I had the right profile for the job, because of my appearance and discipline, and suggested I take a specific course. The salary was about 80% higher. On impulse I took the course because I wanted to earn more money. It would also be good to leave the car ramp as it was now causing pains in my poor legs. I attended the 16-day course and learned a lot about the military regime they imposed. We even sang the national anthem every morning. A good thing, by the way. I finished the course with another vision for my life and work made clearer. I realized that my objective was my well-being and not only the money and I thought the security job would not make me happier. In addition, I would lose opportunities of practicing my English with the guests. So, I said no to the offer of promotion at the hotel.

Chances

In my bellboy uniform!

bit.ly/1x2P82m

The funniest part of my life at the hotel happened when David put me up for a promotion as a bellboy. I later became known as the hell boy! The interview for my promotion was very funny. Juliana Schievano was a new supervisor at the front desk and did not know me. When I went to apply for the job and I received an interview, I spoke in Portuguese. The supervisor asked me to continue the conversation in English. I kept talking in English at the same speed I had been talking in Portuguese. I hope you don't mind me saying that she was very impressed and so recommended me for the job.

The new position made me feel even better. I knew, however, that I would need to improve my spoken English and decided to take a course offered by the hotel at no cost. For some time I attended two free courses at Senac and Renaissance. My classmates were some of the hotel directors and I began to see people as they really are, flesh and bones, like myself. Two people on the hotel course were special because of their humility: Jorgiane Machado, a teacher, and Lúcia Leite, a director.

Renaissance trained me to provide good service by letting me experience many different services. I am not an arrogant man for I am conscious of who I am but I believe that I learned to behave as a true citizen because of the positive approach and great training I received at the Renaissance Hotel. They allowed me to see excellent theater plays. They gave staff birthday dinners, with permission to take some of your own relatives and friends along. I even received massages in the hotel SPA, premiums for being a good employee. Nowadays I can sit in the finest restaurants of the world feeling confident and comfortable knowing that I know how to fit in.

From the very beginning, I volunteered for every training course the hotel offered. By learning so much I reduced how much time I spent on the valet parking ramp. Many of my valet parking co-workers did not seek out training opportunities. I also got a lot of value from many other training courses outside the hotel. As an associate to the Union of Hotel Workers, I played in the soccer games and got to know about still more courses. Among them, one about Management and Governance and another for bartenders. These courses helped me to achieve another promotion into the department of banquets. At that time I was beginning to make plans to sail the seas of the world.

So I had different phases in the hotel. I started as valet parker, then became a bellboy and later a bartender. Each one of these phases was extremely rewarding but the job I enjoyed most was being a messenger. The way I lived at that time would certainly make a fine Hollywood screenplay. All the messengers worked hard but were always in a very good mood. One of the

João Reis and I at the Renaissance Hotel Xmas party, 2008

Natal 2008
14 de Dezembro de 2008

83

RENAISSANCE
SÃO PAULO HOTEL

reasons for our well-being was because of the leisure activities that we had in our spare time. Almost every evening we gathered in the Japanese Bar, our temple to drinking. We had permission to use a football field rented by the hotel every Saturday afternoon. We made paint ball wars. We also organized some barbecue parties at the best steak houses of São Paulo without any cost to us. In addition, the hotel promoted parties at the end of each year in wonderful farms located in the inland. All of these events provided many happy moments for all of us who worked there and contributed to our spirit of good service to the hotel.

The call of the world

The year of 2008 arrived. The hotel about which I had dreamed so much was already becoming smaller in my perspective of life. I had other projects in mind.

One day during the chats that happen between the concierge and bellboys when no one has anything to do, I told Suelyn, a nice girl who worked with me, about my desire to work on ships. I knew she had worked on-board a ship once and I asked her about life on ships. She told me that life is not easy for the workers due to an intense and stressful routine. But in her opinion it was worth it because of the money and opportunities for gaining life experience. I got curious—it is my nature—and asked what I should do to apply for a job. She gave me the address of a shipping agency in the seaside city of Santos. She advised me to do extensive research before applying because it is a complex world and I should be fully aware of what I was going to face.

I went home burning with curiosity. Immediately I opened Orkut, Brazil's answer to Facebook at that time. Marcela, God bless her, had built a page for me a year earlier. I started to make my travel plans. I found some forums where people discussed their experience as ship workers. For months I did my homework and I discovered a position for a bell attendant, considered one of the most difficult tasks on-board. The bell attendant could never disembark to enjoy visiting the ports because on the embarkation days he had double duties always carrying luggage for passengers up and down the gangway. Certainly it would be a different routine from the one I currently had at the hotel. There I had an eight-hour shift, which meant I had an easy life. I searched some more for an easier job and found it working in the ship's bars. I would benefit from a better wage and from more time off to visit places when the ship docks.

This meant that it would be a much nicer life. Taking into account that the two things I like the most are travel and hospitality, I decided to become a bar waiter. However, in order to do so I needed to have relevant experience.

I had to move fast, so I looked for a free course for bar waiters at the Union of Hotel Workers. I took the course, indeed, but after finishing it I needed practical experience. Therefore, I applied for a job in the hotel's Banquet department. I knew the place quite well, the bosses had a good impression of me and it was not too difficult to get a position. I was assigned to the Havana Club, a bar and tobacco store in the hotel. I learned how to prepare and sell the most popular drinks. At the Havana Club one colleague of mine said to me, "If you want to work aboard, do it while you are single". That was exactly what I intended to do. In the meantime, of course, I still worked in a way to enjoy my current job as much as I could.

In April, 2009 I said goodbye to the Renaissance Hotel. Where did I go, when I left that dream?

To live another dream…

Persistence pays off

vimeo.com/115609942

Third Part: Via the Seven Seas

Chapter 13

Preparation to embark

On March 30th, 2009 the shipping agency sent me this email: "I confirm your date of embarkation is April 12th in the ship Voyager of the Seas. Departing from Galveston, Texas."

Reader, can you imagine my emotion? During the year that I had begun the selection process, many things happened. All of a sudden, such a beautiful message appeared in my in-box.

Along with joy, doubts came. My friends and relatives asked me questions that, somehow, made me insecure. "Who suggested you take the job?" "Do you know anybody who has worked on ships?" "Do you know where you are going to?" "Are you sure that this is not a rip-off?" I heard many things such as these. Anyway…

I was 29 years old when I finally embarked. After 15 hours flying, waiting and stopovers at airports and about one hour more in a bus, I arrived at the Galveston Port. I could see at a distance that iron giant; I hadn't imagined it would be so huge. In the beginning it was quite scary. However, I was seized

by other sensations more urgent than the fear. I was tired, hungry and stressed. I was completely dependent on somebody else and did not have the slightest idea of what was supposed to happen to me next. It was my first time overseas in a foreign country. The longest of my trips before this had been the bus ride to São Paulo. The day was cloudy in Texas, by the Gulf of Mexico. A moist breeze blew from the ocean, the remains of a hurricane that had passed by the region some days before. Galveston was devastated. The vision of the wreckage made me evaluate life and many other things from a different angle.

My house of steel

For the following six months the ship became my house, my home, my universe, my portable moving Boninal. It was hard at first to grasp that now I was part of the crew of a cruise liner.

Inside the ship, the crew, people from more than 50 countries, were busy at work. It was like being on a floating United Nations with 1,200 crew members and 3,200 passengers. Each week the liner made a stop somewhere and practically replaced the whole crew. There was never time for farewells. Indifference ruled in the ephemeral and superficial relationship between passengers and crew members, and that situation impressed me. It was so different to what I'd known.

On that first maritime trip, I stepped onto the soil of 40 cities in 18 countries. I suffered; I learned; I exchanged experiences with a variety of people. I was surprised. I was touched, deceived, frustrated, and annoyed. I reached the limit of my sanity, to the point of getting close to abandoning everything and going back home.

Nevertheless, I had joys. I saw fantastic places. I had funny, curious, and surprising situations, from simple ones to the most tense. I saw famous people with whom I never imagined that I would ever be in such close quarters with. I met people who, consciously or unconsciously, gave me support to overcome sensitive moments.

I survived. Six months later, in an ending different from the one I had imagined, at the Barcelona port, I left the ship. Here I am, now, with the mission of reporting everything I've been through. I thought it would be my sea of opportunities. I will tell you more about it, but I first need to write about my journey to the big boat as part of my great sea adventures.

Rowing through life

While working at the Renaissance Hotel, as a bar waiter, I was at the same time preparing myself for work on a cruise liner. Of course I did not know how to do it, so I trusted and relied on my intuition and determination and, in particular, I asked many questions. So many questions that I bored people. Now I know that working in ships is not just a matter of preparation because theory and practice are two different things.

I started searching the Internet. Through the social network Orkut, I found former crew members and spent many hours chatting with them. I obtained the addresses of two shipping agencies and sent my resume to both of them. One of the agencies readily approved me for the position of bell attendant due to my past experience. I agreed, although I wished to be a bar waiter. Anyway, I would take anything to have a paid traineeship. From my research I knew the job was difficult. I did not care. In any case, I went to the second agency. When I arrived there, I found a large group of young fellows, all fluent in English, with college degrees and full of energy. I observed each one of them, fearing them to be unfair competition. Someone was lecturing about the difficulties of life on board. I entered. Finally, the interviewer called my name. Before meeting the interviewers everything had seemed simple enough because when writing a resume we tell only the best about ourselves, but in front of the interviewer we feel naked and weak. I was so nervous. However, I already had a job offer at the other agency and was not too intimidated.

While I waited, I talked to a desk clerk there, Diego. He had been working aboard liners and coincidently also in the Renaissance Hotel. He told me to highlight my knowledge of beverages if I wanted to be a bar waiter. He also told me that, if I passed the interview, the following one would be more difficult, and it would be with the Royal Caribbean representative. Diego calmed me down by reminding me that the Royal Caribbean is an American company, just like Marriott, owner of the Renaissance Hotel.

The result was an email, some days later, calling me for an interview with Douglas, a Royal Caribbean representative. I was apprehensive. The job was not only the opportunity to travel the world without spending money, but also a chance to save money to start my own business as I'd long hoped to have my own hotel. I had to go several times to Santos, 60 miles away from São Paulo, paying fees for lectures and courses they told me to attend. It did not matter. I wanted to get a job on a liner so this meant I spent some of my savings to do the necessary trips to the interviews.

As a precaution, I did not stop the selection with the other agency. The two processes ran simultaneously. I was a little disappointed when the agency gave me an interview for the position of bell attendant. Luckily, though, the second agency assigned me an interview, for the same date, at a different time. Curiously enough, both interviews were meant for the same company and with the same interviewer, only in different cities. I shall explain. The Royal Caribbean was recruiting crew members in Brazil for their 23 ships. Douglas, the company representative, was responsible for all the interviews. What a situation for me! At the meeting in São Paulo in the afternoon I was applying for the job as bar waiter. At the morning interview, I was applying for a position of bell attendant. I had to make a quick decision, so I gave up the morning interview. Even so, with my lack of experience in bar work, I was afraid I would fail. I had no one to talk to and share my uncertainties and doubts. I might not be approved in the afternoon interview and lose my chance because there were 30 competitors. On the hot Monday morning, São Paulo ignored my anxiety and kept its routine.

I arrived early at the office in São Paulo center, drank a strong coffee and waited. This could be the only and last chance of my lifetime. From the "Good afternoon" to the "Goodbye", the conversation was entirely in English. I was so nervous that Douglas said that he perceived in me a certain difficulty of expression because it took so long for me to answer. He asked how I would behave in a situation like that with a passenger. I said I was actually nervous but the reason was that I considered this interview to be the best opportunity of my life, that I was a hard worker and he would not be disappointed if he decided to hire me. Douglas was a very serious man and did not seem to be moved by my words. At the end he said that I would receive an answer by email. I left the office with my heart heavy and my head full of doubts.

The following days I kept checking my emails to see how I went. At night I chatted with some friends I had made during the selection process and all of them were as anxious as I was. And the email did not come.

One night I was in my apartment chatting on the MSN with another Marcela, also a candidate for a crew member. In the middle of our chat, an email message arrived in her in-box. She had been hired and was just cock-a-hoop, pouring joyfulness at my computer screen. I was happy for her but at the same time a little envious because that could be a sign that I was not chosen. My bad feeling lasted for just 15 minutes. I received the message that would change my life forever.

"I confirm your date of embarkation for April 12th in the ship Voyager of the Seas. Departing from Galveston, Texas."

I jumped. I screamed. I was euphoric. Nobody in the house could understand my enthusiasm. I explained, almost crying, that I was now a bar waiter on one of the ships of the Royal Caribbean.

What now? The dream was coming true I thought. Now, I would embark and be happy. Right? Wrong! Now the most difficult and expensive part of the process was beginning. My passport to me is precious like a jewelry box. We get used to everything, to suffering and to happiness. Please read on to know why.

Preparation

I will summarize the bureaucratic process because this book is not intended to be a handbook for sailors. My objective is to tell you my story. Everybody has difficulties but on a ship, the problems are very specific. Any person can overcome those problems with perseverance, competence and seriousness. I did.

If any of the readers need advice, you know where to find me. I will always be available to help anyone who wants to live the adventure I have lived.

Lessons

The *first* lesson I learned sailing, was that working in a ship does not mean being a tourist. We work hard and time off is at a minimum. I had to content myself with a few hours to enjoy the Pyramids or to "hold" the Tower of Pisa.

The *second* lesson is that a first-time shipper is literally alone. Away from everything, he does not know anyone, has no friends and is subject to international laws that he does not understand. And it is not possible to give up and get off the ship in the middle of a voyage!

The *third* lesson is to be sure to prepare yourself very well for the position you chose. There is no tolerance at all for errors.

The Royal Caribbean demanded that we take a one-week course on maritime security, the STCW *(Standards of Training, Certification and Watch Keeping)*. This is a training course accepted by 130 countries affiliated to the International Maritime Organization. The training is mandatory, for instance, for companies that operate along the Brazilian coast for more than three months. The most annoying part of all was certainly the whole set of medical exams, more than twenty in all. We had to be given vaccines for tetanus and yellow fever; there was no choice in the matter. I understand the importance of not risking anybody's health, but I have to say that the procedure is annoying. The marathon of interviews associated with all this is also very exhausting. The

next step was to obtain the work visa in the US Consulate (C1/D category). This kind of visa is required for any crew member assigned to cruises to North America, as I was. I have to say, however, that I did this with pleasure. I felt like the boy who got his first bicycle and did not care about falling off. In fact, I think that falling is a way to move ahead. For me, at least, it works like that.

The date of embarkation was almost here and I was full of expectations. I would leave São Paulo for Miami International Airport on April 10th. I said goodbye to my friends at the Renaissance Hotel at a farewell party they organized for me. It was as if I was someone who was entering a spacecraft for another planet. My family prepared another party, at Aunt Nadir's house, with a nice *feijoada*. This is a wonderful dish made of black beans and pork meat.

So with the blessings of my friends Fábio, João Reis, Caju, which means cashew, and her fiancée Fernanda I was to fly on the first leg of my journey. It was my first time in an airport and I felt very insecure, but I found a friendly man who helped me. I followed his instructions and headed towards the American Airlines boarding area. As I entered the plane, a surprise awaited me—I met several people that I knew. Working at the hotel I had made the acquaintance of pilots and flight attendants who were hotel guests. I made several friends, one of them the Argentinean Tomas Korman, a good soccer player. We just do not agree when he says that Maradona was better than Pelé! I immediately recognized my friend João Pimenta, one of the flight attendants. Very elegant, sympathetic and handy, he told his colleagues to treat this Renaissance bellboy well. I felt at ease. Later, João came to my seat bringing me sandals and champagne from the plane's First Class! Better than that came, he took me to sit in a vacant seat in First Class. I enjoyed the flight sipping champagne! Amazing, memorable things coming my way already in my early days in hospitality!

STCW Fire Fighting Course

USA work visa

Brazilians everywhere

Brazilians are like pigeons ... they can be found everywhere. On the following flight from Miami to Houston I happened to meet Jorge, a talkative and charismatic fellow from Rio de Janeiro. By the end of the two hours of flight I knew his entire life. I still remember an historic September 7th—Brazilian Independence Day—when he gave us an excellent samba show in our crew bar!

At Galveston, a ruined city because of the hurricane, everything impressed me, especially the way people talk so fast. At the hotel I was booked into a room with another Brazilian, Eduardo Monteiro. Lucky for me because he had worked on cruise ships before and so he was able to give me important advice and information.

The next morning, very early, we took a bus to the port where the giant ship was. Along the way, I took in whatever I could from the many sites, sounds and encounters. Nothing more natural it seemed given that I was a Down Street boy on American soil!

Chapter 14

Unveiling mysteries

Many of you certainly know the world that I am about to describe; some of you have heard about it, and a lot of you will never know what there is behind the doors of a cruise ship. I guess that many of my readers do not imagine the complex day-to-day workings of a cruise ship. This is the reason why I will present a brief overview of my first impressions about work on a ship. Privileged impressions, excuse me for saying so, coming as it does from an insider through first hand experience. You will see that there is a certain degree of suffering as well as pleasure. I confess that I do not know how passengers feel from their experiences, so I will restrain my comments to that of the crew member's point of view.

Do not, however, pity me nor think that I am a poor little fellow. Work does not kill anyone, and I am not a lazy man. Besides, I am healthy and vigorous; therefore I manage to overcome obstacles with work and courage.

Working on a cruise ship is something that divides my heart. On one side, achieving my financial objective had led me to this world and it is a pleasure to travel around, seeing the world and meeting people, without spending money. On the other hand, this is something that you cannot do forever if you are wanting a proper family life and to maintain friendships well.

I must admit that I had thought about giving it all up at certain moments. When, however, I found out that this feeling affects 99% of first-time shippers I stayed put. The food is different, temperature varies greatly and add to this large doses of cultural shock. Also my personal history would not allow me to give it up, given my friends and relatives' expectations along with the opinion that all the expenses to date could not just be thrown away and so on. Everything led me to especially consider the financial aspect. I could not go back home with empty hands. I was not the irresponsible adolescent anymore. I used to be though, during Carnival celebrations in Brazil. I needed to plan my future. Leaving the hotel Renaissance had to be worth something.

It was tempting to just enjoy what the world had to show me. But I was no tourist. For me, there was the tough routine of a crew member, ten to twelve hours a day, every day of the week for six months without a single day off. That was the reality. We were there to work, not to have fun. Of course, with some "flexibility", but always respecting the rules, we could escape the routine every now and then and enjoy an exotic world that most of us only know through TV and movies. Shipping companies know that it is not humanly possible to spend 180 days working without any leisure. That is why they do not prevent us from some moments of relaxation. One place where we gathered around for this was the crew bar.

Living the life

Everything that happened to me, at that time, was new, unknown, surprising and enchanting. Paradoxical feelings filled my heart. It was a new life, absolutely unlike my previous life. Magnificent experiences that contributed to building the man I am today. I do not regret anything. I do not lament anything. My many experiences in many ways have brought about my current attitudes and approach to living. The experiences I had on a ship were my experience, and certainly not equal to anybody else's experiences—even a person who had a life history similar to mine, traveled the same ship, or performed the same tasks and lived with the same expectations. Each person reacts in a different way. That is why each experience is unique.

There are people who will never adapt successfully to the routine of working on a ship, especially because a ship may seem to have no routine whatsoever. Some people would go crazy living on that traveling island. As I said, each person is different from another. Therefore, what I am about to tell you is my exclusive experience on ships and in the world, without half-truths, with no grievance or diluting factors. You are going to read about my own perceptions, filtered only by my memory. I will write about the truths that I believe, and I believe them because they are mine. No truth is absolute, as we know. In addition, everything in life has a price to be paid. Knowing the world without spending money may cost you much in terms of work, anxiety or agony. Whether this price is high or low, it depends on our expectations according to one's life experience, cultural heritage and dreams for the future.

Like most Brazilians, I have come from a regular family, as all of you know by now. I was not born with a silver spoon in my mouth, but I was not born in a manger, either. My hometown is modest, counting on one dentist and one midwife. With the help of those two people, I was born healthy and kept all my teeth. Could it be a miracle? I think so. There was for sure a series of lucky factors that allowed me to reach the point where I am today and share my experiences with you, the readers of my book.

Albert Einstein was very wise when he wrote the lines below. It illustrates my own feelings, and that is why I take the liberty of reproducing his verses here:

There are two ways of living life: one way is believing that there are no miracles; the other is believing that all things are a miracle.[1]

---

[1] http://pensador.uol.com.br/frase/MjU5NTA4   Date visited Feb 1st 2015

Chapter 15

First impressions as a crew member

Three buses were necessary to get the 100 crew members to the port from the Sheraton North Houston Hotel where we stayed for the night. I was astonished as I had never seen so many different Asian nationalities together at the one time. The majority were from the Philippines while others were Indonesians and natives from poorer Asian countries. In fact Japanese workers are uncommon in ships.

Would it be pretentious to say that the sky is the limit? But the sea, the sea, the sea, she is not? When I first saw the iron giant full of lights, full of people, I trembled. More than five thousand people in one boat. It took me a while to assimilate that new reality. I followed the group of crew members, dumbfounded, feeling so small before that extraordinary metal monster.

The ship had docked at dawn, after a cruise around the Mexico cost. We waited in line at the port. Geraldo received us, speaking lousy English. He was a tall Mexican man of about forty. He was responsible for the bar department. An ill-tempered man, a nasty host, exhibiting the appearance of a person who had taken all too many tequilas the night before. Even so, with the life manners of an ogre, he welcomed us and took us to an office that served as his personnel department. One by one we handed over our documents: passport, medical exam reports, international vaccination card, STCW certificate. All went by truly fast and tightly organized; they could not waste time because the ship would sail by 5pm. I was among the 100 crew members boarding while at the same time, hundreds of crew members were disembarking because their contracts had ended.

Each one of us signed a contract for either six or nine months. A contract though can last longer—or end earlier—according to the needs of the company. A contract regulates the agreement between crew member and company. We proceeded in single file to embark. Before entering the ship, every passenger or crew member's luggage passes through an X-ray machine. Geraldo, in a hurry, took us to have our pictures taken for our crew pass, a magnetic card ID that also serves as cabin key and debit card for any kind of expenses on-board. It is also a legal ID in any ports where the ship docks. Always rushing, Geraldo explained a few things about work schedules and on-board security. He gave us a stack of documents that we were supposed to read as soon as we could, a time sheet and identification card. He informed us superficially, about everything, telling us that we were to have training periods during the first week to discuss each subject. Then we received our uniforms followed by a visit to see the medical center, and then the personnel department. It was about time to have lunch so we went to the crew refectory. There are different refectories for the vessel's officers, the vessel's staff—workers from concessionary companies that take care of the spa, the casino, the shops and so on—and the crew members.

The first ship

Inside the ship were more lights and glamour. Everything was charming and, at that moment, all organized, clean, and functional. The reality, however, was yet to come and that reality was work!

With my uniform and ID now provided, I was told to find my cabin. I felt lost inside an iron jungle. How would I find a cabin in a moving city like that? Well, as my mother says, use your tongue and you will go to the ends of the earth. I opened the door to a tiny place, and found Luis Puertas, a Peruvian, already inside. He smiled at me. I said a timid good morning. He answered with sympathy and I noticed right away that he was not a native English speaker. To my query, "where are you from?", he said he was a Peruvian and asked me if I spoke Spanish. I said that I didn't but I promised to learn. And I did; the few things I know of the Spanish language I learned from him. We became friends in no time. Thank God, we Brazilians make friends easily. Luis was already an old sea dog, in spite of being very young, and knew all the ways to a good time in an environment that I did not know yet, but was compelled to understand. He taught me many things. It was easy to like him. He was a calm, honest and supportive man. I felt safe in his company.

During the recruiting process they told me not to carry too many clothes because of the small size of the cabin. Small? They were too kind in saying that. The cabin was, in fact, minuscule; the bathroom, even smaller. Nevertheless, it was comfortable. The cabin I shared with Luis, until he finished his contract and took a vacation, was equipped with TV with international channels and internal channels showing activities on the ship. There was also a DVD set, a telephone set for internal calls as well as for the super-expensive calls that I used to make to Brazil, a closet big enough to hang my clothes, drawers, several electrical outlets, space for stowing my suitcase, a hot water tap, a small fridge and a desk where I put my laptop. To future shippers I say this: if you think about working on a ship, do not forget to take a laptop and a camera—basic kit for travelers, because every minute brings a different beauty to be documented.

Not a lot of space in my cabin!

After our brief acquaintance, Luis went to work. I went looking for the refectory. I had had nothing to eat since breakfast. I knew that I had to be quick because a mandatory training course was scheduled to start soon. Cunard folks call that Training Induction 1. The training lasted about an hour. Some of the officers introduced themselves and welcomed the new crew members. They emphasized security, considering it a priority on-board. The captain, a very young fellow, passed by to say hello and summarized what the others had already told us. He advised us to stay away from drugs and alcohol, inside or outside the ship, since random blood tests would be done from time to time to ensure we were fit to safely perform and carry out our work duties. He said that drinking was not forbidden, but that we should not overdo it, in order to not put at risk our own lives and the lives of our colleagues. Moreover, we had to be ready for work every morning. He warned us that intimate contact with passengers was expressly forbidden. What kind of contact? Touching, kissing, having sex.

After hearing all this I was sleepy and went back to the cabin. The day had been full and it was already 3.00pm. Anyway, there was no time to rest. Geraldo gave me a sheet of paper, my work schedule, and a map with the location of the bar I had been assigned to. Well, I had signed a contract to work, but… to start working like this, without any specific training? That is how it is. A crew member costs a lot for the company, so he has to start working as soon as possible. The future crew member should not be fooled into thinking that life is easy on-board. He will work, as his contract states, between 10 to 12 hours a day (sometimes even 14 hours), without a single day off. A respite on a ship is a rare reward, as I will tell you soon. We do not embark to travel, but to work hard, and bring a profit to the company. We sign a contract, agreeing to do that. So, let me work.

It took me several days to adapt to the reality of the ship. Soon I realized that English was not a strong point of many of my colleagues. There was a mix of languages, dialects and slang of several places in Latin America and the Caribbean.

There were many people who spoke Portuguese on-board. I would like to tell you about some of them.

My first time on the ship

vimeo.com/115331060

Eduardo Monteiro, 24 years old, was not very tall but athletic and handsome. He had previous experience of nine months on another ship and worked in the same department as me. A very cheerful young man, he became my good friend. Jorge Fabiano, 36 years old, skinny, religious and a hard worker, had been a Brazilian marine, but was working as a civilian on ships for the first time. Among the three of us, I was the only one that had never been on a ship before. By the way, I had never even seen a ship. You can imagine my surprise! How could such an iron mountain of 138 thousand tons float? No matter how many courses I took in Brazil, I would never have been sufficiently prepared for such a magnificent vision. The ship, Voyager of the Seas, was built in 1999 as one of the three biggest ships of its time: 311 meters long and 48 meters wide. It was like a 15-storey high monster softly floating the ocean. It had 15 decks, each one corresponding to the floor of a building from my way of seeing it. The 1,557 cabins are structured as apartments as in a hotel—four times the number of apartments of the Renaissance Hotel. This can easily accommodate 3,200 passengers. To serve all these people, the ship has 1,200 crew members and, by way of interest, they were from more than 60 countries. This was the universe I had entered!

My workstation

Back to that April 12th afternoon, with my work schedule and a salver, a pen and a folder. I went looking for the pool bar, my workstation. The pool is on one of the highest decks from where one can get a 360 degrees view. This is especially great when the ship is leaving the port. There was a sail away party to celebrate the departure. The party would begin by 5:00pm and Geraldo recommended that we should look handsome and be scented. Following his advice, I took a long shower and shaved. Wearing my uniform, I lost my way in the labyrinths, but managed to arrive on time at Deck 11. Many passengers gathered there for the party.

I will never forget that first vision of the space that would be my new world from that moment on. I was frightened in the middle of such a crowd, but at the same time, I felt distinguished because the passengers, mostly American, when they saw my uniform, surrounded me ordering drinks. They asked for beverages of which I had never heard! In spite of all the courses I had taken, I had no experience with international drinks.

A new warm feeling came over me. I was fascinated by such unique new things: the sea below down there and the land slowly moving away into the distance. Only people who have worked on-board or sail the seas will have an idea of what I am talking about. It is an unforgettable experience.

In the meantime, I was completely lost with so many orders for drinks. Naturally, I was nervous; it was a new job. But there was something else: I went crazy trying to understand the Texan accent—they sound as if they are chewing tobacco while speaking. My colleagues, mostly from the Caribbean and the Philippines, who prepared the drinks in the pantry, made a fool of me during the sail party. In the midst of 30 bar waiters yelling their orders, I had to guess the lousy English that my colleagues used to name unpronounceable drinks and beers. There was, however, a dose of good will, although sometimes they pretended not to understand what I said just so they could watch me get nervous. It is a real baptism of fire for a new hire. Once more, I survived.

At sunset, we closed the shift because the pool bar did not open at night. My work at that bar would be my daily routine throughout the twelve days of the cruise. After the party, I proceeded with the cleaning: wash the floor, store the fruit and all the materials used during the day, and then organize the clean glasses. A Filipino utility boy helped me. The highest number of employees in every ship of the world are utility boys. We had to be quick with this, because we had to be at the theater entrance soon to welcome passengers—and try to sell some drinks, too! The interval would last an hour, and during this period, we were supposed to clean the bar and, if possible, have dinner. Having finished the cleaning, the first round was concluded.

My workstation!

Now we ran to the theater because the show was beginning. To make money via a 15% commission, I had to sell drinks. In fact, that was my salary. Needless to say that there is a fierce competition among the bar workers. I reached the theater with the help of Gary, a pantry boy. Tired and a little scared, I marveled at all that beauty. I was seeing, for the first time, the space reserved for passengers. It was like a shopping center full of cafés and bars, including an English pub and a champagne bar. In the middle of the main square was a wonderful red automobile. It was a luxurious environment; enormous, where everything works perfectly. There are infinite options of entertainment for the passengers and the schedules are strictly followed.

I started working. However, being simply a beginner among 15 "sharks"—so called because they are experienced bar waiters and good sellers—in a theater full of people, I was not able to sell anything at all. They knew the terrain and knew how to behave to succeed. I would learn in time. Well, since I could not sell, I watched the Broadway show. So I can say that the night was not completely lost. I had to wait anyway, to clean glasses and the mess. Beginners suffer, that is a truth. But even suffering ends. That first day, at midnight, was finally over. In fact, not the day, but the shift. My crew members' social activity was about to begin.

A day that almost did not end

I do not need to tell you how tired I was at the end of that first day. So before going to bed I decided to pass by the refectory to eat something. There I met Eduardo, who from now on I will refer to as Dudu, and Jorge. We talked about my experiences that day which they had no idea about because they served in different bars. Dudu convinced me to accompany him to the crew bar to meet the "paisanos" (Italian word for compatriots). It is a good way to make people meet their fellow country-persons. Jorge preferred to rest. I was tired, but wanted to know all I could. Besides, I had heard about that bar, considered the most amusing spot in the ship. We went to our cabins to change clothes. Dudu knocked at my door half an hour later and showed me through the labyrinths—I would certainly not have been able to get there by myself. The bar was a hidden place with windows to the ocean. It was a sight to see at night.

I entered the crew bar. I would go there many more times, after that. Dudu introduced me to a bunch of people, without ceremony. I felt welcomed and the place was good for a dose of freedom and comfort. It is an enormous hall capable of holding 1,200 persons, with a big bar in the middle, where one can buy spirits, beers and cigarettes. Smoking is permitted by the open windows. There is a pre-paid Wi-Fi Internet connection, video games, pool tables, and a store with basic hygiene products and instant food. At one corner, there is the so-called staff bar for the contractors (people who work in the casino and spa, for instance). At the opposite corner was the officers' bar, for the officers and people with military rank. Those two bars are not so much fun though, and many times the officers, and even the Captain himself, joined the crew members for a drink.

My intention was to have a beer and a talk about so many new things I had experienced that day. The major part of the gathered group was formed by first timers like myself. But pay attention to this warning if you are a candidate to work in a ship: the crew bar is highly addictive: every night there is something nice going on and because of that it is always full and amusing. But even so, there is work the next day…

I left the crew bar to finally go and get some sleep with Dudu showing me the way. Once one understands the logic of a ship it becomes easy. Crew members stay in wings, or stairways, according to their occupation. Each group stays in the same stairway. The idea is to put all those together who follow the same schedule, preventing disturbances and allowing for maximum rest and sleep. Crew members cabins are located in decks A, B and C, below the waterline, therefore without windows. Depending on the cabin location one can hear the waves crashing against the ship. I lived once in one of those cabins. After my first impressions, the jet lag, the long flight hours and the work, I was beaten by tiredness and was soon in a deep sleep.

Overview of the ship

I have written about my impressions in relation to the "Voyager of the Seas". Now I will write about the general peculiarities of a Cruise ship.

First question: *Can a crew member get off the ship in any harbor?*

Yes. That is how, by this time, I had taken more than 40,000 pictures throughout the world. Anyway, each case is unique, and the authorizations may change according to the department where the crew member works. Some jobs allow more free time, others do not. Do you remember the research I made through the Internet before choosing the bar department? I did not seek work based only on wages. I selected the position that would give me more opportunities to see places I wanted to see. The crew member needs a crew pass, the ID called a Laminex, supplied by the security department on the first day, to get on and off the ship. With that Laminex I could visit Mexico and the Caribbean countries. It is the same in Europe, and there Brazilians do not need a visa. Everything is simple, but temporary disembarkation can be made only during rest time, and rarely longer than a few hours. Remember: we do not have days off: we have only time off. Sometimes we leave work by 5:00pm and the next work schedule starts the next morning at 9:00am. Therefore, this means we have only a free evening.

To get off the ship in American harbors, besides the Laminex, the crew member has to fill in the I-95 form, a special authorization granted by the US Immigration Department and not easy to obtain. Once on American soil, those who have not yet got the necessary landing card are conveyed to the Immigration Department for an interview. Some colleagues of mine had to wait for up to four months to get the I-95. I was lucky—they never once refused me a visa. Every time I go to the United States I disembark without any trouble. I understand the inflexibility of the US Immigration Department though. A former colleague, Nick, a Filipino, very easygoing, 30 years old, and a male nurse who graduated in Manila—he had the I-95 visa. One day the ship stopped in Los Angeles, coming from Hawaii. Nick got off the ship and never came back again. According to some friends, Nick had met a cousin who was already living illegally in California and decided to stay even without his passport, which was kept in the ship. People from the Philippines, as I said, are the majority on ships, almost always occupying junior positions, as in cleaning, for example.

Second question: *Is it easy to make friends on-board?*

Let me put it this way: 60% of the crew members are Filipino; the other 40% are from other nationalities. In numbers, people from India come next, working in all departments. The other nationalities vary much from company to company. Here, at Cunard, Philippine people are also the majority. Latin American persons are not many; I would say less than 50 in total. We Brazilians number just twelve. Lately, I have seen an increasing number of East Europeans working for Cunard. There are Ukrainians, Macedonians, Serbians, Romanians and Hungarians, all very much alike physically: pale, blond hair and light blue eyes. All of them are very professional. Many other nationalities can be found on-board, with only few representatives, sometimes only one: Italian, Australian, Japanese, French, Chinese (Mainland China and from Hong

Kong), Uruguayan, Thai, Guyanese, Peruvian, Argentine and Nepalese among others. I am very curious about different cultures and I enjoy making videos. Therefore, I decided to make a video that includes all these nationalities. I had thought to have a short interview with each one of them, asking why they chose to work on a ship. This would be a herculean task, so I recorded 60 colleagues, just identifying themselves and saying hello to the camera. The video turned out to be a success on YouTube. I will write more about this video in the next chapter.

Third question: *How is the training?*

In the first two weeks, the newcomer participates in training almost every day, with the emphasis on on-board security. One of them is the boat drill, which involves training for emergency evacuation of the ship. This training may happen twice in the same trip; one involving crew members and passengers, in the beginning of a cruise, and a second one in the middle of the trip just for crew members. Passengers may participate in the second training if they wish but only a few of them do. I got lucky again: all the training sessions happened during my work hours—Safety Induction 1, 2 and 3. The training hours are registered as working hours, anyway. No one, I repeat, no one, can miss those training sessions, no matter what! Safety is the most important thing on ships throughout the world. Those training events are exhausting.

Evacuation training

Fourth question: *Is the food for crew members different from the passengers' food?*

As I said in the beginning, food can be good or bad, depending on the crew member's usual habits. It is not as bad as they say, but it is not as good as the traditional Brazilian rice-and-beans dish. As I mentioned earlier, there are some days when the food is so yummy that we think it might be passengers' food. On other days, however, there is only sticky rice and pieces of strange meat. Desserts, nevertheless, are always superb: great cakes and pies and a lot of ice cream. There are themed parties, with delicious food and sometimes an American barbecue. At Cunard, food is great, and once in a while the ship's personnel manager promotes parties like Cheese Night or a Pizza Night. That makes you forget the regular food.

During meals, I have seen bizarre scenes—bizarre to me, anyway. People from other cultures have different habits; I understand that. But it is quite strange to see people eating with their hands, instead of using forks and knives. On the other hand, people may find it unusual that we Brazilians share a 600ml bottle of beer with three people—the same amount in England, for example a pint, is usually for one person only. So I rather respect the habits of others and live well in the community allowing each to his own way of life.

Fifth question: *How do you communicate to the rest of the world?*

On the ship, crew members can buy an international phone card for a reasonable price. The duration of the card depends on where the ship is, but in general it lasts 45 minutes to one hour. The connection is usually good, although the signal may happen to fail. You use the phone in the cabin to comfortably talk to your family. The company always provides a free card for a new starter to call home on the first day. The card for Internet access is expensive. It costs twice as much as the phone card and lasts between two and three hours. We prefer to use free wireless connection when we get off the ship, in the bars close to the harbors. My advice again to candidates for crew members is this—always take a laptop with you. At the crew office, we can buy a SIM card with an American phone number, in case we need to call home. In Europe, I am able to use the Internet with my Blackberry mobile and send messages via BBM (BlackBerry Messenger).

A tough beginning

Now that I have highlighted those important considerations, let me go back to that first trip.

After two days, we reached the second country. I could not get off the ship. In the first week, we went to other Caribbean countries, but I could not get off the ship in those either. I remember well where and how I spent my first three hours ashore. In Cozumel in Mexico, I do not lie by saying that I did not go far from the ship—I was afraid that they would abandon me in that place so far from Boninal. I stayed at a distance of about half a mile from the ship but enjoyed a cold beer and took hundreds of pictures. I guess that taking pictures of nice places is a way to capture and take reminders of places that we might never see again.

The first weeks on-board were harsh. Several training sessions, long working hours, daily pressure for results. I had some dog days, and thought about giving up everything. But, then again, I was in a place that hundreds of people would like to be, thanks to an opportunity I received from God. I had to earn and make the most of it.

Fortunately, the first cruise leg was over. Looking back, it passed quickly.

Bound for Europe

It did not take long for a reward to appear. It was summer in the old continent, so it was time to follow the winds in that direction and cross the ocean to Europe. We left Galveston, Texas, bound to Southampton, England, in 14 days. Every four sailing days the ship made a stop. The first was in Bermuda, more or less in the middle of the Atlantic Ocean. We remained there for 10 hours. Since my shy promenade in Cozumel I had been on-board for two weeks and was truly in need of fresh air—I could not stand the on-board air conditioning any longer. I plucked up my courage and invited my cabin mate, Luis Puertas, to go out and visit the British island with me.

In fact, working for Cunard, I would go back to Bermuda two more times. The clear sky, reflected on the sea, painting it blue by the beautiful Horseshoe Beach. It was a wonderful sight that gave me strength to go back to work again. I found it very strange that the steering wheel of the bus was on the right side.

The amazing Horseshoe Beach

bit.ly/1x2Udri

Those crossings are tough for crew members. They last eight to 10 days, passing through the Bermuda Triangle, a place of heavy seas that make the tasks of a bar waiter very difficult.

On one of those days, I made a very embarrassing mistake for a bar waiter. I was working at the Cleopatra bar in the vessels' bow. Deck 4, I think. Every day, in spite of the ocean conditions, there was a party specifically for passengers who had made the crossing before. Those frequent travelers had the benefit of drinking and eating canapés and snacks at no cost during the whole trip. The young Canadian captain participated in those parties to shake hands with the VIP passengers who were either silver, gold, platinum or diamond members. One day, while he was addressing a speech to the audience gathered around a table, I was serving a martini to a chic American lady at that same table. Maybe I was seasick, I do not know. What I know is that I dropped the tray, with all the drinks, over the lady. To add to this, it was right in front of our beloved captain. I cannot avoid this joke: my name is Martinês, so it is natural that I drop martinis! The woman was extremely kind. All wet and messy, she kept repeating to me: "Don't worry, don't worry, son, that happens". In fact, I was not worried about her. I was terrified by the looks of the captain and the officers. As Andy Warhol predicted, I had my 15 minutes of fame—but I would rather not have it. Anyway, luckily everything ended up fine.

Four days after this terrible event, still sailing by the scary Bermuda Triangle, we reached the Portuguese island of the Azores. A pretty and clean place that I would visit many times. My first time on Portuguese soil had a special enchantment for me since we are very alike in cultures. However, speaking Portuguese out of Brazil, being so far away from home, was somewhat funny. The other crew members flattered me because I could understand the natives. The Azores people are humorous and I spent a nice time on the island. I would find, two days later, that Lisbon people are no different either—I spent a very nice day in the Portuguese capital. Feeling self-confident, I invited my friend Jorge to visit with me. Portugal colonized Brazil in the 16th century. We took a train downtown. We had only a few hours, but it was enough time to visit some tourist places. One of them was the statue of John I, in whose name the island of Azores was discovered.

Jorge had taken a camera that used acetate film. I remind you that at the time of the trip, 2009, digital cameras still were not as common as they are nowadays. I had a super camera that I bought in the United States. Jorge was not happy at all with the fabulous pictures I took with my camera and considered that I was trying to humiliate him and his old film camera. He was upset for two days but finally forgot the whole thing and now we are very

Jorge in Portugal

good friends again. He indeed was my tour guide when we visited the city of Rio de Janeiro, where he was both born and now has his home. Anyway, Jorge got angry and went back to the ship. I decided to do something I had been planning to accomplish for a long time. I went to a small restaurant where the food was cheap, as was the hygiene, and ordered codfish, the national dish, and rice from a mustached Portuguese.

I gave myself forty minutes to enjoy the meal, taking advantage of my solitude to think about my life on-board. It had been a month since I had embarked. Life was getting better and my fellowship with my colleagues was getting more positive. After a month, everything becomes clearer. One enters the eye of the hurricane and thinks that is normal. I was building good friendships, first Dudu and Jorge, then some others became friends too. Angelo, for instance, is a great friend. He was the one that put me forward for a fine job in São Paulo, at the Unique Hotel, when I went back to Brazil. But I will write about this in another chapter.

Let me write more about Angelo now. He was born in Belo Horizonte, in the state of Minas Gerais. He was 25 years old, at the time of the trip. Skinny, charismatic, he spoke fluent English. He knew the ship very well because of his job in room service. He used to say that his first contract was going to be the last. He has kept his promise, so far.

In Europe, we lived for a few hours of amusement and high emotion. The ship was in the port of Cobh, in Ireland, most of the passengers had left for a walk and so the work diminished. We were all crazy to enjoy a day of rest. Angelo invited a group of five Brazilians, including me, to visit the town of Cork, one hour by train. The train was clean and fast. The day was cold, but at least it was not raining. We had time to take the train at noon and be back on the ship by 6:00pm to depart for Cherbourg, France. In Cork we visited a medieval castle and had lunch in one of the shopping centers; we were tired of the food of the ship. Since it was pay-day, we had money, so I bought a shirt showing the flag of Ireland and drank the famous Guinness beer. So thrilled were we that we lost all notion of time. When we realized that the time was running away, it was already 5:00pm. We ran to the train station to find a long line of people—it seemed that all three thousand passengers had decided to take the train at the same time. We entered the line as if we were passengers and managed to get on the train. The carriages were as crowded as the São Paulo subway in rush hour. Fortunately, we arrived at the ship on time. The cruise continued.

Next stop, Cherbourg. In that town there is a memorial to the ship Titanic, with a replica of the famous English vessel, because Cherbourg was the penultimate port where Titanic picked up passengers before the tragedy. The port is beautiful and modern, with the neighborhood keeping the traditional architecture of the 19th century.

That was that. We arrived at Southampton next, the port closest to London, and the home of the Titanic; today, the home of Cunard, the company I have been working for over the last three years. It was a morning in May 2009. Southampton was an unknown port to me. Now I have lost count of how many times I have been there.

I woke up early to work on side jobs. When we sign the contract, there is a clause which stipulates that we have to comply with a work load of X number of hours per day, including some tasks different from the one we are hired to perform, such as loading luggage in the elevators on the boarding days, storing boxes of beverages, wheelchair assistance to passengers in need. On boarding days, all crew members work a lot, and it is practically impossible to escape from side jobs. Generally, we arrive at the port by 7:00am and by 4:00pm everything has to be completed for the new cruise. Every crew member is involved in the process. I had survived days of rough sea, a tray accident, almost missed a train in Ireland, but I arrived to the land of the Queen of England full of happiness and not even the side jobs could take away my good mood. My duty was to convey wheelchair passengers to the place at the dock where buses and taxis waited. I enjoyed doing that because it gave me four hours of work and then a break of four hours. After that, we traveled to Germany where the ship was going to stay in maintenance for 13 days. That is what they call dry dock. I will tell more about it shortly. I worked at a high pace, but very carefully. After all, I was taking care of elderly people in wheelchairs. I was feeling happy about helping people that could not walk. Moreover, I knew that after that day we were going to have 13 days of rest in which to get to know Germany.

My excitement was visible. I performed my duties with such happiness that at least ten old fellows generously tipped me. I remember a nice woman that gave me all her Euros; she told me that the currency in England is the pound and she was not in the mood to change her money. By the end of the four-hour shift, I had lots of Euros, pounds and dollars in my pocket. And my holidays were just beginning. Before the departure from Southampton, I had time to take a walk in Southampton. It was very nice to see and photograph those famous red double-decker buses, true postcards of England.

The ship left for Hamburg. The sea could not be better. The weather was cold, but we were relaxed. We organized a party to celebrate the ship without passengers. The next morning we still had to wake up early, but the shift, now, would last only six hours per day. At deck 11 we did all the tasks relating to the dry dock. Slowly the giant entered the dock canal. By then the bar department team were storing tables and chairs from the pool bar and, from up there, we had a fantastic view of Hamburg. It was a well-planned city and very clean. I was so anxious that I could have jumped in the River Elba and gone swimming to find my freedom and a beer.

Many other ships were entering or leaving the port of Hamburg, one of the largest ports in the world. By the canal margins, we could see glass fronted shops where call girls exhibited their personal attributes. A paradise for sailormen.

Dry dock

I have not yet said what a dry dock means. It is the situation where a liner or any other ship is compelled to remain in a shipyard for a period for repair or maintenance. This is usually for a period of 10 to 20 days in general, or even months, depending on what needs to be done to return the ship to good working order. I have been through two other dry docks, in 2010 and 2012. Dry docks are mandatory every two or three years for most ships. I call those dry docks "lucky dry docks", because without passengers the workload diminishes quite a lot. In addition, the crew members can take advantage of the period to make cheap tours, since Brazilians do not need a visa to enter any European Union country. All three dry docks in which I participated happened on German land, twice in Hamburg and once in Bremen. I know many experienced crew members who never participated in a single dry dock.

Oh yes, I was lucky, indeed. After a month and a half of embarking in Galveston, I received the gift of a glorious vacation in Europe. I remember something that I read somewhere:

> *A man needs to travel. On his own, not through stories, images, books, or television. He needs to travel for himself, with his own eyes and on his own feet, to understand what is his. So that he might someday plant his own trees and value them. He must know cold in order to enjoy heat. And vice versa. He must experience distance and homelessness in order to feel at home under his own roof. A man needs to travel to places he does not know; he must lose the arrogance that causes him to see the world as he imagines it, rather than simply as it is, or as it can be; the arrogance that turns us into professors and doctors of what we have not seen, when we should be students who simply go and see.*[1]

[1] Amyr Klink, Endless Sea: Alone around Antarctica—as Far South as a Boat Can Sail, trans. Thomas H. Norton, English (New York: Sheridan House, Inc., 2008), 69

Gosh how I love these lines that Amyr Klink wrote! I wish I had written them.

Thus, the giant stopped in the dock. For us, it was an extraordinary chance to see naval engineering. The first interesting fact was that, when the ship entered the shipyard, the dock is obviously full of water; it has to be lifted for the water to drain away and the sight of the hull, which usually stays underwater, is impressive. After eight hours pumping water, the ship is put on easel stands—imagine a 138,000 ton ship supported this way!

Ship out of water - a rare sight!

Once the ship opened its gangway, a real party began. All the crew members spread out to the streets of Hamburg, for their very own and personal "dry dock" experience. During these 13 days I got to know the city of Hamburg really well. Luis Puertas and I visited the main monuments as long as the admission was free, because we did not have much money. We visited the old train station. At the city library we spent hours and hours using the free Internet. We used the subway to go everywhere, and I would learn the main differences between Germans and Brazilians. At the subway station there are no turnstiles. We bought tickets on the first floor and then validated them in one of the machines on the boarding platform. I did not see anybody checking tickets on the train. Yet everybody had paid for their ticket. How different it is in Brazil!

We used to go out at night to a bar, where the Beatles had performed their first time in Germany back in the early 60s. We gave a show of our own to the audience there when our friend Joelma stepped up on the stage and danced the samba—the Germans just loved it! The Port of Hamburg was completing its 820th anniversary, it was built in 1189, and the celebration party took the whole month. We could not, and would not, escape from the two unforgettable weekends we had complete with plenty of beer and food. Even though I saw quite a few people drunk there was not a single fight or disagreement. German people behave well and enjoy parties. What I did not know was that the party was just an appetizer for the biggest of German parties—the Munich Oktoberfest. I had the opportunity to spend five days in 2012 at that party—and what a party that was!

Dry dock is a harmonious period for crew members and their bosses. In our parties at the crew bar even the officers abandon their strict behavior and had fun with us. The Panamanian, Rufino, my supervisor, always so serious, danced his traditional salsa like a ballet dancer with an Ecuadorian who worked at the reception desk. They received thunderous applause from the entire bar department. We, warriors of the sea, had days of delicious amusement and fine rest.

What is good, ends too quickly

The dry dock was completed. We only had time for one last party in the bow, with an American barbecue and free drinks. Then the ship, smelling brand new, left the calm waters of the river Elba to go to the Mediterranean.

Our next stop was charming Barcelona, a beautiful city that will remain forever in my memory because it was the base for our ship for the next four months. Even with only two hours of rest on Sundays, I always managed to ride my bike for a "cafesito" at my favorite bar. The cycle lanes of Barcelona are the proof that there is a solution for healthy travel in big cities.

It was time to go back to work, because the Mediterranean Cruise season had begun. All crew members were re-invigorated. I, for instance, was prepared for new towns. After a while, I must say, the routine gets boring. It is not haughtiness; the thing is that routine kills the imagination and repetition kills surprise. After a time doing the same stuff all over again, one gets sick even of beautiful things.

For four months we made the same seven-day cruise several times and rarely did the captain alter the route. The passengers changed every Sunday in Barcelona. It was my favorite city of the itinerary because before boarding the new passengers I always found time to ride my bicycle through the city. Sometimes Angelo and I rode by the beach to have lunch and a Spanish "cerveza"—a Spanish beer. All very enjoyable!

On the Cruise, always the same six places, we left Barcelona and traveled one day to Naples, Italy. From Naples to Civitavecchia, the port nearest to Rome. The next day we went to Livorno, also in Italy, the fastest way to Pisa and Firenze. Every Friday we stopped at Villefranche, France, a beautiful town, close to Nice and Monaco. And last we went to Marseille. We usually left Marseille early, around 4:30pm—our usual daily departure time was 7:00pm—because the nautical distance was long and ship travel takes time. If I had to write about all that happened in each stop, I would have to produce a few more books. Anyway, I cannot shirk telling the funny or remarkable stories of each day of the week.

Monday

... a hard workday, but even so we found a way to have some fun. It is hot in Europe in June; therefore, the pool was always crowded and we had work all day long. At night, however, we would party to get rid of the tension. We promoted our crew parties on Mondays because it was the day before the first stop; we know that the passengers would be excited to visit the first port next day, and the ship would then be empty. Therefore, we could party until dawn.

Tuesday

... in Naples, was a day for pizza and the local beer, the Birra Peroni. Naples is very similar to some Brazilian cities, especially the traffic. The Neapolitans sell whatever you want to buy. They are famous for being the first in Europe to acquire modern technology. João, a member of the ship tour office was a graduate fellow who knew Naples quite well. At that time, Apple had just launched the iPhone. João got excited and bought an iPhone for 90 euros, a nice price; the lowest cost we saw elsewhere was 300 euros. Back to ship, he opened the box. Inside the box he discovered just a bar of soap. Yes, João had bought a bar of soap for 90 euros! There are people in Naples who are very fast with their hands. Here is a piece of advice to anyone who is intending to visit the island of Capri or Vesuvius: think twice before buying an iPhone.

Wednesday

... was the day dedicated to a small town with a big name: Civitavecchia. As I said, it is the port closest to Rome. It is a bustling port, all year round, because Italians of many cities prefer to embark there. I normally made my phone calls and money transfers to Brazil in Civitavecchia, because they have a friendly system. From there I went twice to Rome by train; it takes one hour and there are a few services per day. Talking about trains, I met a

Brazilian family on the ship. Father, mother and three kids all on vacation together. They decided not to pay for the excursion organized by the ship team and left early to take the train. Even without speaking a single word of Italian they managed to get to Rome. The next evening I met them and asked about their tour to Rome. They said it was a disaster. They misunderstood the train schedule and missed the ship. Conclusion: they had to pay five more train tickets to reach Livorno the next day to get on board again. It was useless to complain, because the ship has a strict timetable to obey. In case of delaying to set sail, the company that owns the ship has to pay fines up to ten thousand dollars, depending on the port and the country. I do not defend the price of excursions organized by the ship, but it is advisable for passengers not to risk independent adventures. The ship excursions are safe and never leave passengers behind!

Thursday

... was the day to take advantage of the free internet at the main square of the port city of Livorno; there was nothing else to do in that place. At my first opportunity, I went to Pisa, to see for myself the place that puzzles so many people. It was amazing in the beginning, but Pisa did not impress me as much as other Italian cities such as Rome and Firenze (Florence). Firenze is a city to visit more than once. As for Pisa, I was quite satisfied with the pictures of me holding up the leaning tower with my hands.

Friday

... we docked at the penultimate port of the cruise, Villefranche. Disembarking was exotic, it was the only place where we went to land by tenders, small inflatable boats. The beach is small and shallow so the ship cannot go near the coast. This French village is a magnificent place. We, Brazilians back home, could hardly wait for Fridays because, when the weather was clear, we could watch the girls go topless. For me, a country boy, it was a spectacle. Villefranche is close to Nice, a place that I also visited, and less than twenty minutes away from the Principality of Monaco—a place I have been dozens of times. Walking through the narrow streets of Monaco, I saw the highest symbols of material wealth, and I remembered the races of Ayrton Senna, I felt like I was 15 years old again, watching the racing cars and dreaming of driving one of them. To visit Monaco was a great joy to me.

Saturday

... last day of the cruise, was celebrated in the city of Marseille, one of the biggest in France. I liked to walk in that city because the food is good and public transportation is efficient. I visited the soccer stadium which is both modern and beautiful. The port, however, is distant from the city and, as we had to leave by 4:30pm, there was never enough time to enjoy the various places on offer. My friend Jorge went out in Marseille and did not read the schedule in the ship's daily program. He thought that, as in all the other ports, the departure would be at 7:00pm. Poor Jorge. By 5:00pm, he found only a port agent in charge of delivering his passport and money for a ticket to Barcelona. In the meantime we worried about his disappearance. He showed up the next morning happy as never before. He had to make a train connection and while waiting he met people who are still his friends today.

Bound for Europe

vimeo.com/115331057

Misery

I said earlier that the four months in Europe were boring. That's not completely true. I adored each town, each port. The problem was the price of everything. Europe was in the peak of the economic downturn caused by the US real estate crisis. In that season, almost all passengers were Spanish who had bought cruises at the price of bananas. They did not spend money, and bar waiters became distressed over this—we were on commission. This meant, no drinks sold, no wage! My salary, in dollars, was less than what I earned at the Renaissance Hotel. Anyhow, I honored my contract until the end. Dudu could not handle the lack of money and gave up, right before completing six months. I thought I was doing well, selling more drinks than he did. I had learned to sell, after what I had experienced on my first day. In fact, I was making only enough to pay the expenses charged by the company. Royal Caribbean discounts from our salary, the cost of uniforms and the value of plane tickets from our country of origin. Not to mention that, in Brazil, I had to pay for medical exams, courses, visa, everything. Therefore, I made special efforts and, even in the middle of experienced crew members, I sold enough drinks to pay my expenses and to save some money to take back to Brazil. Not much though, I must say.

Before I left the ship, on October 4th, 2009, many things happened. My buddy Luis Puertas left. In his place came a young Brazilian college teacher, Kyvy, who made my last two months on-board very happy. Another good friend was Fernando Monteiro: a handsome, funny, polyglot. By then, he was dating Simona, a gorgeous Italian girl, to whom he is married today, and they shared a cabin. On a certain occasion, three girl friends of Simona embarked for a short cruise, paying a symbolic fee of US$10 given that they were friends of a crew member. Fernando had to give up his place in the cabin for the visitors and asked to stay in our cabin. The cabin, as I have already told, is extremely small; we spent seven days in a tight space. It was fun though. We kept telling jokes all night long.

When my contract ended, I left Royal Caribbean. I found out that other companies existed that allowed me greater opportunities for more varied and professional experiences. Royal Caribbean, for my career though, was a worthwhile watershed and became a turning point for me. I said goodbye to that company on a Sunday morning in Barcelona.

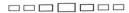

Chapter 16

Planning the next step

"You leave the ship, but the ship does not leave you." I do not know who said that, but it is very true.

Back to Brazil

I arrived in Brazil with two fixed ideas. First: I would work on a ship again. Second: I would try working for a different cruise company.

Before finding another job, I decided to visit places within my own country. When abroad, I had received a lot of questions about the Amazon Forest, about Rio de Janeiro and many other places. I was embarrassed to confess that, being a Brazilian, I did not know any of those places. Therefore, I decided to take a national tour.

Most crew members, when they leave the ship, get the impression that prices in Brazil are low, because they calculate everything in dollars and Euros. The same thing happened for me. I found a promotion by a regional aviation company and bought a ticket valid for a month, paying US$250 in cash. Mateus, a friend I met on the ship, joined me. However, we had just forgotten to calculate the cost of hotels, taxis and food!

We stayed in the Amazon for seven days. Then we traveled to the north-eastern regions of Recife and Maceió. Now I had something to tell my on-board clients about Brazil. And, very importantly, now I know that Brazil has so many natural beauties that need to be both seen and preserved.

Creatures of the Amazon: pythons, caymans (crocodilian) and sloths

Although a little disorganized because of the little money I had left, the trip ended in my own state, Bahia. There is an eroded land-form there, called Chapada Diamantina, something like Mountain of Diamonds, with beautiful waterfalls, trails and caves. This is a place that has given me such peace of mind that one can clearly perceive the presence of God in nature. This is a truly blessed piece of my country.

I wandered throughout Brazil for eight months.

I am like a gypsy in relation to jobs. In that eight-month period, I worked as many things. I was a recreation monitor at the time of the New Year's party. I then worked for a month in the pet shop with my friends Tiago, Tavinho and Alessandro—I really do not like dogs, but I needed the money.

I think I was not born to stay put in one place. This is likely to mean that I will never be employee of the month in any company!

Planning the next step

I praise the coincidences of life. In the case of the Unique Hotel, the building looks like a ship. After working in a ship, your life will never be the same again. Mainly because of the large number of people that you meet along the way.

As I always say, a good friend is better than money. Thanks to Angelo, I was hired at the Unique Hotel, where I had some of the happiest moments of my professional career so far. I am a very lucky man. I have been in the right places, with the right people, who led me to the right places. How could I not be grateful to someone who helped me secure a job? Angelo did this, when he introduced me to Victor Siaulys, the owner of the Unique Hotel. The hotel is a family enterprise and Victor told its history in his book "Mercenary or Missionary?". It is a bedside book for anyone who dares to take risks and succeed. Every employee should read that book or at least the chapter that tells the hotel's history. In ten pages, Victor manages to give a clear overview of that giant embedded in the middle of São Paulo city. Besides all this, the view one can enjoy from the terrace is fabulous: there are no other buildings near the hotel and you can see the Ibirapuera Park with all its trees and lakes, a peaceful spot in the heart of the urban jungle. At sunset, when the city lights come on, the landscape is even more beautiful. Working there was, for me, a pleasant professional and personal experience. During those four months working there I made exceptional friends. Working at that second "ship", I started imagining myself being the proprietor of my own hotel. I knew that working in São Paulo, where 50% of the wage goes to pay taxes, transportation and meals that I could not yet have done that. I talked often to my friend Bambam about my dreams. He was a bartender like me, at the hotel. Today he works in a Royal Caribbean ship, thanks to the advice that Angelo and I gave him. I said many times to Bambam that my dream was to go back to the seas, but this time for a different company.

I was 30 years old and had six months experience on a ship. I did not want to take any more false steps. I would go back, but only to work in a bigger liner company. After all, I had all the skills that a cruise liner company demands.

Back on-board

I passed through simultaneous interviews in two of the most respected companies associated with maritime cruises in the world. The process was the same I faced the first time. I applied for jobs through two agencies and each one made an appointment for an interview. Both companies approved me: Crystal, one of the top five of the world, and Cunard, perhaps the world's most traditional ocean liner company.

Some days after that I received an email telling me to get ready to board in July on one of the Crystal ships. However, by then, I had fallen in love with Cunard and their Queen Victoria liner. And so I decided to wait. It was worth the wait: On May 3rd, 2010, with great joy, I received a message that said that my date to embark on Queen Victoria was set at June 14th, 2010. This was even earlier than the Crystal ship's start date.

One month and a half later, I disembarked at Heathrow Airport, in London. Cheeky as always, I checked in at the airport hotel. For the next five hours, I could do whatever I pleased and decided to go for a walk. I visited Big Ben, at the Palace of Westminster and walked the streets of London. I assure you that London is the one place in the world where the ancient and the modern are most harmonious.

In front of the hotel at Heathrow the next morning, the bus was waiting at 7:00am sharp, on time as all the British are in my opinion. Our destination was the city of Southampton. On the way we passed beautiful landscapes with a lot of green and all around seemed very well organized. We got to the port right on time. I already knew the ritual—where to go and what to do. On the Queen Victoria everything was impressive. I had 17 days training, the White Star Academy, during a cruise to Venice, that was fundamental for me to adapt to the logistics of the company. Of course, not everything is like "la vie en rose", but I am glad to say that there were many flowers lining up for me. On my resume as a tourist, I already had visited 18 countries. Cunard literally took me to the rest of the world. Norway, Egypt, Russia, Greece—the cradle of western civilization. These countries are very special to me because of their beauty and specific characteristics. The photograph on this book's cover, for instance, was taken in Geiranger in Norway. This is the closest place to heaven to me.

Heaven on earth

bit.ly/1zeRml4

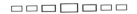

Ancient temple ruins, Greece

The Great Pyramids, Egypt

Chapter 17

In the wonderland

How could I not love Cunard?

Of course, everything has a price to be paid. But I am willing to pay every penny for this dream…

Work, and the reward will come

Finally, I reached the peak of my professional life. The almost bicentennial British company, Cunard, owner of the three most famous cruise liner ships of the world, was going to celebrate its 170 anniversary the following July. This meant a terrific party during the nine days cruise around the United Kingdom. My ship was the Queen Victoria, named after the queen that ruled the United Kingdom of Great Britain and Ireland between 1837 and 1901. There are two other ships with the names of British royalty: Queen Elizabeth and Queen Mary 2. I would also take part in the Jubilee celebrations in June 2012. This was to commemorate Queen's Elizabeth II's 60 years of reign. The three Queen ships departed together from the port at Southampton. I was in the party who nominated the current commodore of Queen Mary 2, Christopher

Rynd. He is not only commodore of Queen Mary 2, but of the three ships at Cunard. I saw the Royal wedding of Prince William and Catherine Middleton on the huge screens installed in the vessel, along with everybody celebrating with champagne. And how could I forget the first female captain of Cunard ships, Inger Olsen. During the Olympic games in London, I was on the Queen Victoria. I have been privileged to see many historical events while on-board.

Queen Victoria, in relation to the other ship I worked on before, was smaller: 294 meters long and 90,000 tons of weight, so practically half the size. After three years working on Queen Victoria, I can say that it is a magnificent ship. Inaugurated in 2007, it was still looking brand new by the time I embarked. It counts on almost the same number of crew members; 1,000 in total, which is just 200 less than in my previous company, to serve 2,000 passengers. Each crew member serves two passengers, and guarantees the service of excellence. In the 12 bars on-board I make sure my clients, the passengers, are treated and tended to like a child is by a babysitter.

There is a rotating work schedule, well organized and fair enough for every one of the bars. On each cruise the bar waiters are assigned to a different bar, since some are more crowded than others. Thus, by the end of each month, the bar waiters are in an all-win situation. At Cunard, the percentages of sales are distributed equally without all the crazy competition that I witnessed before in my earlier job. In each of my four contracts with Cunard, I have been able to save five times as much money as before. It has been the best job I have ever had, and I hope you can grasp how proud I am of working for Cunard.

Here, two pieces of advice if any of you are intending to work on-board. Firstly, if you are not happy on the first ship you work on, give yourself a second chance as it could be the chance of your life. Second, never mind the figures in your bank account before you check the fringe benefits too: no rent, no bills and a great opportunity to know wonderful places. In a way I can consider myself a millionaire—I receive a salary to travel. Is that not great? Besides all that, at Cunard everything works to a British clock. I have learned discipline. I have made money as I have never made before, because I had no expenses and therefore could save a lot. With the money I saved, I was able to buy a partnership in a hotel near São Paulo city—São Caetano do Sul.

Even being the sea of opportunities that it has always been for me, São Paulo educated me for the world. And it has succeeded. I have a motto: *whoever lives in São Paulo city is capable of living anywhere in the world.*

But it was with Cunard that I managed to reach my goal of traveling and saving. The company is so organized and offers all the opportunities for one to work. Another bonus is that I find the environment both tranquil and pleasant. Queen Victoria, in a manner of speaking, was like a holiday camp to me, when comparing my previous work experiences. Of course, I had some disappointments, especially because of the differences among ships that I had to come to understand. My focus, however, was being happy doing the two things I do best, travel and serve. I feel I have accomplished these well.

A ship pays tribute to the past

Most of Cunard's guests are British, because its home is the city of Southampton, one of the most famous ports in Europe. All decor of Queen Victoria resembles the RMS Titanic, as one can see in the pictures throughout the ship. Paintings, chairs, chandeliers, every detail reminds me of the British movies of the early 20th century.

The ship's theater has a box that was inaugurated by Prince Charles and Camilla, Duchess of Cornwall. I had the pleasure to sit there, once, to watch an Irish musical, an opera, as a reward for outstanding sales. There is also the Queens Room, with capacity for 800 people. This is where the ship's main events are held: The Captain's party and masked balls among others. At those events, one can see "the gentleman hosts", men hired by the company to dance with unaccompanied women.

Everything on-board has the British touch. Decoration of the bars, casino, spa, the artists including comedians, pianist, harpist and musicians in general, genre of music—absolutely everything is designed to the British taste. There is a division of guests in categories, according to the cabin they occupy. We see this at the restaurants. The fanciest are the Queens Grill and the Princess Grill. As well there is the Britannia Club and last, but not least, the Britannia Restaurant. However some passengers like to eat at the Buffet. There are some areas restricted for those who pay more to enjoy privacy and exclusivity. This is one of the company's defining standards.

A married couple, both Brazilian doctors, took a fourteen-day cruise on the Queen Victoria. They paid a considerable price and so had the right to enjoy everything on-board. One day, the man needed help to telephone his daughter in Brazil. He asked me to help him using the telephone card because he could not at that time get assistance from the reception desk. Always obliging, because that is how I am, I helped him to contact her and he then talked to his daughter. The couple could not get assistance because they did not speak English. That is the main problem for Brazilians who travel on the Queen Victoria. Therefore, here is another piece of advice: get prepared and learn at least basic English: everything on-board is written in English and all the announcements over the loudspeakers are made in English. Since Cunard does not sail to the Brazilian coast, native crew members are very few and far between. In my time there were only 8 Brazilians among a total of 1,000 crew.

Crew member respected

It is only right, and a matter of justice in my opinion to praise Cunard for its remarkable organization. Being the most famous and historic of all names within the shipping and cruise liner industry, Cunard Line has acquired a fantastic expertise that makes everything on-board look very easy.

I did not have to pay a single penny to embark and begin work. From the uniforms, washed and ironed every day, tickets for planes from and back to Brazil, hotels, medical examinations, work visa, to even a telephone card I bought at the airport for an emergency call, the company reimbursed me for every expense I had. In addition, we can use bicycles free in any port of the world. As I say, the company pays me to work and, indirectly, to follow my dreams of being a tourist.

I'll explain. In each port, the company organizes excursions for the passengers with outsourced companies that work onshore. Crew members are invited to supervise the excursion services as tour escorts. I was always volunteering because, without the need to pay for it, I could live a passenger's day! I was visiting places without worrying about the time and expenses, eating and drinking as a passenger. As a tour escort I visited the Egyptian pyramids, the city of Meteora in Greece, the Geiranger fjords in Norway, New York and many more places of great interest. In turn, I think myself lucky to have those opportunities. I talk to a lot of people and I learn different things and points of view, and I get to see the world. I also get to know each place in a particular way. This extra job is not for everyone though.

Occasionally we also have crew-only tours organized by the company. It is inexpensive and always to exotic and hard places to reach. I have been to many places on excursions like those: Jerusalem, the North Pole, and Rome, among others.

Pleasant routine

At the present time, I am serving my fifth contract with Cunard. The company makes its best efforts to guarantee the crew's welfare. Payment is good and in relation to health and nutrition, we are almost like the guests on the ship. I feel at home, as if we are a family. In those themed dinners I mentioned earlier, sometimes senior officers such as the hotel manager, the maître'd, the personal manager and even the Captain (the Master) show up to serve us. At those moments, they show their human side. The ship life, day to day, has a routine and may oblige senior staff to be cold.

I took the advantage of the company's good will and, as a good Brazilian, took control of organizing soccer matches inside the Queen Victoria. With the help of the very capable personnel manager, the German Carola, everything was easy. Of course, it was nothing like our matches by the banks of Cochó River of my childhood, but nevertheless it had its own magic. I allowed myself to feel like a professional player in Denmark, Norway, Italy, Belgium, Malta, Ukraine, Grenada, Greece, Aruba, Portugal, and Mexico... A football match is the best way to feel at home, because the language of the football is even more universal than the English language!

My beginning with Cunard was much easier than at the previous company, just one year earlier. I was not thrown to the lions on the first day. To the contrary, I had 17 days of training—White Star training—to learn all aspects of my work before going into practice. I learned about the history, the philosophy and the policies of the company. During the training I shared a comfortable stateroom with David, an Englishman whose home was originally Southampton. Thanks to that respectful and supportive beginning, I could develop into being one of the best sales people on the ship.

The crew cabin I was transferred to at the end of the White Star training was small but comfortable. We had a DVD player and a TV, a telephone and a small bathroom. In that cabin I had several different companions along the way. This was because sometimes we are assigned to other decks and have to move to be in the same bar area. The first was Oleg, a 45 years old Ukrainian who loved Brazil and Brazilian women—he would say this every evening after drinking a bottle of vodka! One Swiss fellow, however, was special.

Peter Stilhart, 53 years old, was a short skinny man and a bar waiter like me. Everybody was very fond of him. He had been working on ships for 28 years. Can you imagine all the stories he told? Peter loves Brazil and his favorite place is the Amazon region. We shared a cabin twice during my four contracts. Being the older inhabitant of the cabin, he had the privilege to choose the low bed of the two bunks, but he gave it to me without any problem. Among the many conversations we had, one of them led to me thinking about my future. After a few shots of gin, his favorite drink, and almost in tears, he told me about his German friend who decided to quit working in ships in 1988 when they worked for another company. This friend suggested Peter stop too because, without a routine together, it was impossible to have a family. Peter listened to his friend and meditated on what he was going to do with his life. Today, 2013, he continues working on Queen Victoria. He has two kids with different women: a gorgeous girl in Thailand, whose picture he always exhibits, and a boy somewhere else. Peter spends his vacations with a girlfriend from the Philippines. He advised me many times to save my money and invest it in real estate, since life on ships can be short.

Intimacies

The story of my friend Peter leads me to answer a question that might have crossed your mind. Is it or is it not allowed for crew members to have intimate relationships amongst themselves? Of course it is!

Think about it … six, eight, sometimes ten months away from home. It is almost impossible to resist. I say almost because I know many people who did resist. In my case, it has been impossible so far. There are many couples that have been formed and got together on the ship, some of them sharing the same cabin. Married couples have priority in sharing cabins. But there is no impediment to moments of intimacy with whoever wants the same. I started working on ships in 2009 as a bachelor and I met a beautiful girl called Alice working on-board from Northern Ireland. There is an important rule however—crew members must stay away from passengers. Always, in fact!

In June 2010, by the time Brazil was shamefully eliminated from the World Soccer Cup in South Africa, as a soccer fan I discovered some other things of the British culture. One of them is that the British are as passionate as Brazilians for soccer. However, they call it football or the beautiful game. During the matches, the British watched TV at the on-board pub, called the

Golden Lion, drinking as much as a Brazilian would do. We increased drink sales very much during that World Cup. In general they had fun; their happiest moment was the elimination of Argentina from the championship. I don't know why they don't like the *hermanos*—the name we call Argentinians by. Their time came, though: the English team lost to Germany 4 to 1. After that, they cheered for the Brazilian team. With all that was going on in the guest social areas, in the crew bar the debates and bets were hot. The majority considered Brazil the favorite to win, remembering the past. To tell the truth, I thought Brazil could win the world tournament. In fact, I dreamed about it, and had a lot of fun with representatives from all the other countries. In the end, when we were eliminated in the quarterfinals, some crew members looked at me as if they blamed me for the loss. An Italian man was upset because Brazil lost the game. For me, patriotism makes me feel guilty sometimes, but luckily I get over these negative feelings.

After the World Cup the work on the ship was still frantic. We started a nine-day cruise to nine cities of the British Isles and one French town. It was a special cruise because of the company's 170th anniversary. It was a pageant cruise with, again, most passengers from Great Britain. The ship departed from Southampton and stopped first in Cherbourg, France. Then we journeyed to Cobh, Dublin, Belfast, Greenock, Queensferry and Liverpool, home of the Beatles. In Liverpool, we had Camilla Duchess of Cornwall on-board, for a solemn ceremony, and a Beatles cover band playing for the passengers. The ceremony was special to me because I could witness the prestige of Cunard. When the ship left Liverpool it was loudly acclaimed by the public with large crowds cheering us off.

If I could express here the impressions I had of each country I visited, and the sentimental values they represent to me, I would not have enough space to write everything. Russia, Panama, Estonia, Finland, Sweden and the other 80 countries, and more than 300 cities I visited. Nevertheless, in these brief memoirs of mine, I just want to emphasize some dreams that came true. Egypt is in first position. Norway, for very different reasons comes second.

Kissing the Sphinx

bit.ly/1zeTc5t

How do we celebrate birthdays on-board?

My birthday is August 8th. On that day in 2010 the ship was at the port of Saint Petersburg, Russia, for an overnight stay. I was in an excellent mood, and had adapted well to life on-board. The itinerary was perfect: a cruise to the Baltic Sea. There were many beautiful girls on-board. I was just loving having reached my thirties as a bachelor. I was not involved with anyone at the time. I must say this though, on a ship, a relationship is not recommended.

When sailing, birthday parties take place in the crew bar, with the type of music chosen by the birthday person. Everything is allowed for the birthday person but, even so, they have to be aware of their work schedule the next morning. I have seen many crew members warned for oversleeping after a party night. A different thing happened to me.

The morning after my birthday party, I could not get up for what we call cabin inspection, a weekly routine for checking hygiene and security. My shift would begin at 1:00pm but I was supposed to be up by 10:00am for the cabin inspection. My manager came to my door, but I had forgotten to set the alarm and had not woken up. My bar manager gave me a scolding and reprogrammed a new inspection, telling me I would get a warning if I missed it again. With three warnings a crew member can lose their job!

Let's go back to the parties. When we are lucky enough to be in the right place, a birthday party will be even better. That specific night was the most outlandish of my life and I will never forget it. Many of us went to enjoy the Russian nightlife, since the ship was going to stay at the port for two days. It was not at all a regular night: it was my birthday and I was in Saint Petersburg with an entire night to rest. I gathered some of the few friends I had made in the first two months on-board and we got off the ship. We totaled three Mexicans, one Englishman, and two Russians: Pavlo and Marcha who served as tour guides and interpreters. I found very few people speak English in Russia. That day, however, I would not mind the language barriers. I only wished to party in the land of vodka and beautiful women. The two Russians were not so friendly, because that is how they are, but they were very handy. They knew that it was my birthday and took us all to one of the best nightclubs in the city. I drank champagne and ate caviar for the price of a second-rate meal. Some beautiful blonde girls took us onto another place and we went back to the ship at 8:00am.

Nights out

In my early days on the Queen Victoria, I had some overnights out too. One of them in Copenhagen, a piece of heaven on Earth. Everything works well in Denmark, both in daytime and at night. The problem is that everything costs too much. I remember going to one of the best bars in the city, expecting a happy night out, but my pockets were almost emptied. Just to give you an example: I collect shot glasses and I buy one in each country I visit. Usually I pay US$3 to US$5 dollars for one of these glasses of spirits, but in Copenhagen I spent US$14. Imagine the rest…

One of the best nights out was in Amsterdam in the Netherlands. The prices were lower than in Denmark, but even so we had warmed up in the crew bar before going out. It was the night of August 28th, 2010, and a Saturday in Amsterdam, the city where everything is allowed. I left the ship after 10:00pm, earlier than usual because I was working at the café, where the shift started earlier and ended earlier. My work schedule for the next day would start at 5:00pm, so I had all night to enjoy this bachelor's paradise. I went downtown, about twenty minutes from the port, by myself, because my friends would be working until late. I preferred not to wait because I did not want to lose a single minute of my time in Amsterdam. We agreed on a meeting place, but I would not see my workmates again that night.

I made the obligatory route for any tourist in Amsterdam: the traditional Red Light District, a street full of glass fronted shops where prostitutes show their attributes—just as in Hamburg in Germany. There are many bars, side by side, bathrooms without doors where people relieve their needs without caring about who is passing by. Inside the bars, marijuana is legal to smoke and can be purchased as if it was a regular cigarette. Once I satisfied my tourist's curiosity, I got to go to one of the ten best nightclubs in the city called "Escape". I entered, self-assured and free of any engagement. It was a spectacular night. I met many tourists and made friends. A solitary Turkish guy joined me to chase girls and we talked to a lot of girls that night. I spent one hour talking to a Portuguese girl before remembering to ask her where she was from. When she said she was from Portugal, our common language made everything easier. I will not tell how we ended the night, but I can tell you the night ended just fine, thank you very much. It was a magnificent experience being in Amsterdam. It really has everything one hears about and I can testify to that. I have been there more times since, and I have visited many monuments and tourist attractions and tried Dutch food in a big restaurant near the port. That was in 2011, during a period when Alice's family visited the city for a couple of days to visit us.

Who is Alice? I will explain. But first to note that sea and love are treacherous. When we least expect it, someone comes out of the fog of time and, like a wave, floods the heart, drowns our priorities and weighs anchor in our thoughts. That someone was Alice.

Alice ... aah, now there is Alice

Istanbul, Turkey, September 17th, 2010 was the day I kissed her for the first time. My life changed. I do not intend disrespect to any of the good women with whom I was involved before, but Alice represented strength and profoundly affected my life. Even today I can see the good that results from our relationship. Alice was the most ardent supporter of my idea to write this book. Before I tell you what happened between us, I have to introduce her.

Three months after I embarked on Queen Victoria, Alice embarked as a crew member, to work in the shops on-board. It was September 11, nine years after the attack on the Twin Towers in New York. A ship is like a small town. Everything happens fast and has an immediate impact. She appeared in front of me as if from a lightning bolt from Zeus. I wondered who was this Irish goddess that in an alleyway had interrupted my path and then, my peace. Somebody informed me she had started a six-month contract. Her contract would eventually be extended to nine months, and I am going to tell you why that happened.

I instantly fell in love with her. At the crew bar, feeling shy, I had no courage to approach her. In fact, I was afraid of being rejected in front of so many people. So I decided to wait. But I did not wait long. Two days later, I declared my feelings for her—in a different and not very romantic way, although effective.

It was September 13th. To the contrary of what the popular tradition says, I guess that thirteen is a lucky number for me. Alice was not even aware of my existence, but I had the urge to tell her about my feelings. The next morning, the ship was anchored in Venice—a place where we would spend the happiest night of our lives. Even without knowing whether she liked coffee, I took her a cappuccino in the shop where she was working. It may not have been a romantic approach, but at least I found a way to introduce myself to her. She was surprised by my gesture and did not accept the coffee at first, afraid that the situation would cause her trouble with her supervisor. She would confess, later, that she found my initiative very romantic.

I told her my name and asked something about her. The blue-eyed Snow White, 22 years old, was born in Portrush, Northern Ireland. As she spoke, I realized that yes there is perfection in this world. I could not understand well what she was saying, and I became nervous, and more nervous as I understood less and less. The fact was that I was completely lost in love. We talked for just a few minutes more, because we both were in working hours. But she promised to meet me again.

Three long days passed. On the 17th the ship was in the port of Istanbul, where we were going to stay for two days and one night. I had not seen Alice again and I had forgotten to ask her cabin number. Anyway I made an appointment to meet two South African friends in the crew bar that night but they did not show up because they had arranged dates. So I decided to go and visit Turkey by myself. At the famous Taksim Square, a central point for tourists, I expected to find somebody I knew, which was likely to happen because many crew members had the night off. Indeed, I met two friends. They wanted to take me to an underground place but that idea did not attract me. I said that I already knew the place, said goodbye and went looking for something else to do. It was still early.

Blessed is the time I said goodbye to those fellows. I had barely taken two steps when I came face to face with a mirage, as in a desert, to quench my thirst for love. Alice, the blond haired goddess, was sitting in a small bar right in front of me. I had had other relationships. Somehow, those seemed just like mere attractions. With Alice it was different. I felt my legs shaking, a flushing coming up my neck and I blushed, hot in my face and in my belly—a somewhat nice affliction. I stood still for a few seconds without knowing what to do. She saw me and smiled invitingly. Without thinking I went towards her. She was in the middle of a group of friends from the ship. I did not care. Feeling a little more confident, as we had both talked before, I asked permission to sit by her side. After one Turkish beer and between another, with the wishful scent of strawberries and narguilés, the smoke of the hookahs nearby, Alice gave me a sweet wet kiss. That was a special night. We began a fine relationship. We became true friends. In fact more than that, we became allies. We reached a fine point with each other, tuning into a place where it is hard to trust fully but, at the same time, we hold onto people because of our own needs.

From that September 17th on, my life changed very much and for the better. I focused on my work and therefore I worked better and sold more. They say that love works miracles. When it dovetails, love is even more effective, and in accord puts one on the right track. That is what happened to me. I treated her with respect and she returned this, and my care for her was an unconditional love.

Very well educated, Alice has traveled much, in spite of her youth, and so was as an experienced worker on Queen Victoria. To her, unsolved problems did not exist. I was deeply proud of being with her.

I remember the first night we spent off the ship. We were in Venice. The ship would stay for three days for passengers embarking and disembarking, a routine usual at the end of the year. Alice wanted to do something different to celebrate one month of our relationship and convinced me to spend the night at a hotel so that we could forget about work. She already knew Venice well, a place where she had been on vacation. She booked us a room by telephone, in a marvelously romantic hotel. We checked in at 1:30am and a night of romanticism and pleasure marked our relationship. The next morning, we still had time for a café macchiato and a pizza by one of the canals of Venice. I was supposed to start work at 5:00pm and Alice was not due to work. When the ship is in port, the duty free shops do not open because of local regulations. To end those days of romance, we had a toffee ice cream in Saint Mark's square, listening to violins. It could not have been more perfect.

During another stop, that same month, Alice and I drove a car to Santorini, Greece. It was her idea once again and, after a quick search on the Internet, we had ourselves another special day. We saw the whole island for only 20 Euros. In one part of the island, we found a perfect spot for a picnic. It was an afternoon to make the Greek gods envious of us.

As I said before, everything on a ship happens fast and it is very intense. Alice and I were already sharing a cabin and the relationship would become more serious when a long stay at a dry dock came up in December 2010. Once more by Alice's initiative, we spent one of the best vacations I have ever had in Europe.

The dry dock in Hamburg lasted for 14 days. Alice invited me to visit her home to meet friends and relatives. I did not think twice. She was the woman of my life after all.

She insisted I improve my appearance for the trip. I trusted her so I let her dress me up for the occasion. We bought some new winter clothes in Southampton and she simply changed my style. Looking back now, I can see how much she improved me. She made such nice choices that I have not abandoned the dress style she suggested for me.

We bought airplane tickets to fly from Bristol, where there was a direct flight to Belfast, cheaper than from Southampton airport. We took a train to Bristol, promising our bosses that we would come back two days before the ship departure from Hamburg. Europe faced a harsh winter that December. In Northern Ireland, according to the news, it was the worst winter of the last 60 years. Up to that moment, I had never stepped on a snowflake—I knew snow only through Christmas movies. On the way to Belfast, where Alice's parents would be waiting for us at the airport, I was frozen—by both the cold and my anxiety. I had never before met so formally, a girlfriend's family. And I had never stayed in a girlfriend's parents' house, especially sleeping in the same bed. Maybe the snow made me uncomfortable. But her parents were extremely sympathetic, and they were the best hosts I could have had in Portrush. It was obvious that I was a stranger in the place. My Brazilian skin gave me away, even after six months in the ship without sunning. The town, though, was cozy. Everybody knows everybody. Within two days I felt at home. I visited the oldest whiskey distillery in the world, the Old Bushmills. An irony of destiny: I went to that famous whiskey distillery in 2010, and only in 2013 did I visit a brewery of the famous Brazilian drink, the cachaça. We also visited Eire. In Dublin, I tried the famous Guinness beer with Alice's father. I had to put on a big man's face because the beer is so heavy that it may well have been invented to test a man's masculinity.

The two Irelands are divided mainly by religion. This is an odd thing to me, because in Brazil we respect all religious beliefs and do not care about the differences between them.

We stayed at Portrush, Alice's small hometown for eight days. Then we flew to Berlin where we stayed for four days. It was a place we liked to visit. Again, those were the best of the four vacations I have taken in Europe.

Winter in Berlin

bit.ly/1Eo9FpM

We went back to the Queen Victoria. It would be my last trip of the contract, which ended on January 13th, 2011, in New York.

Still there is Alice

In the two years we were together, Alice and I visited more than 30 countries. We had been through many memorable experiences together and created a history that could compose a book of its own, mostly pleasantly. We rode camels in Egypt, we jet-skied in Mexico, and we bicycled in Nicaragua. The best country though that we visited together was Brazil. We traveled around for a month and I showed her some of Brazil's natural beauty such as the North-eastern beaches and Rio de Janeiro. She came to Boninal with me too.

In August 2011 I brought Alice to São Paulo for a barbecue party at Mrs Cida's place with all my family, including Aunt Nadir and my sister Bila. We also went to a dinner given by my friends Ana Paula and Ricardo, to celebrate my 32nd birthday. As always, it was nice to see them again and be able to introduce my girlfriend to them. Not all was rosy, however. We had some linguistic problems. Alice didn't speak Portuguese and nobody in my family spoke English. Because of this, she could not easily show her charisma and many positive attributes.

We also spent a week in London, this time at the house of one of her childhood friends. With Alice's help, I was able to get to know London well.

One time, in Saint Petersburg, we had a remarkable night. Our bar manager, trying to increase the sales of the department, promoted an internal competition among bar waiters and bartenders of the Queen Victoria. The worker who could sell the most drink tasting sessions would be entitled to a dinner for two at the fanciest restaurant on the ship, the Todd English, and also one night off in San Petersburg in Russia. Of course, I did my best to win. At the beginning of the competition, I along with two other colleagues were in a tied position with ten tastings to each one of us. I sold 29 tastings; the second place had 11. I did not know at the time, but I established a record on the three Cunard ships. According to my manager, as of November 2012, when I left Queen Victoria, that mark was not yet beaten. On two other occasions I also won rewards for sales, but with smaller amounts. When the night came Alice and I went to the Todd English, both of us very well dressed. I do not like wearing social clothes so I put on a dinner suit. Alice was resplendent in a red dress. We ate a wonderful dinner feeling like a princess and her bridegroom, and then went for a walk in Saint Petersburg, finishing the night with a glass of wine.

I also lived splendid days in New York and Cairo on behalf of drink tasting sales rewards.

And yet, Alice

We had our bad moments too.

One of them was in the beginning of 2012. Alice could not get a date to embark at the same time as I did, as we had during the previous contract. It was terrible, because we were apart for five months: I was on the Queen Victoria and she was between London and her hometown. Longing to see each other, we talked often on the phone and on the Internet, making plans. She wanted us to live in London or Ireland. Unfortunately none of this happened because I was too selfish. I would not leave Brazil to live in a cold country. I do not know whether I was right or wrong—time will tell. What I do know is that I did what my heart asked me to do and that was that I went back to Brazil and bought a part share in a hotel. To this day, I remain a part owner in this hotel. It was also my desire to write this book while in Brazil.

Alice and I were apart for so long that the friendship cooled down, and so too our love. After almost six months without seeing each other, Alice embarked on the ship again. Many things had changed between us. We ended up breaking the relationship. Nowadays I think that I am her friend. I have much to thank her for by way of everything she has given and done with me. I learned much from Alice, the beautiful stubborn Irish girl.

I decided to keep away from ships for a time, to relieve emotional stress and to write this book. Alice, if you are reading this, please receive my warmest thanks for the support you gave me in this project.

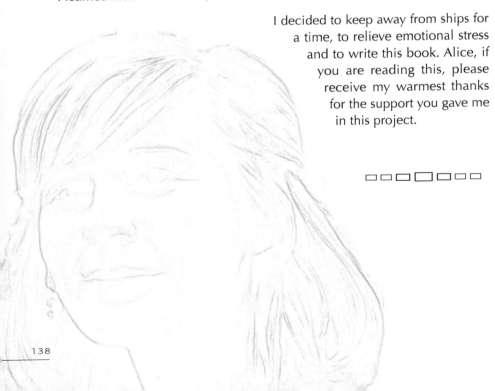

Chapter 18

Victories on-board and on the ground

Alice's absence for those five months, although painful, allowed me to get closer to three nice fellows I met on Queen Victoria who are today my good friends. One is Hector Dorigon, a photographer who works as a bartender. Born in the south of Brazil, in the state of Rio Grande do Sul, he barely shows the typical southern accent. He is clever, sensible and a fine professional. He dates Kaly, a Brazilian girl who was sailing on the same ship we were.

Old and ugly but still my friend!

I first met Hector through the Orkut website in the beginning of 2010 chatting via email. At that time he was waiting to embark at the Royal Caribbean and simultaneously was having interviews for Cunard. It happened that some Cunard representatives went to São Paulo to hire new employees for a new ship, the Queen Elizabeth. Hector and I had the chance to meet in person and I showed him the nightlife of São Paulo. Soon after that I was hired to work on the Queen Victoria. Hector was not so lucky at first with Cunard. But another company did hire him. He needed money to pay his rent, and, though not happy with his contract, he embarked. We kept in touch and I was giving him advice to help him to adapt to the dynamics of the ship where he was working. Almost two months later, he received a call to embark at the Queen Victoria and asked for my opinion about whether he should trade-off companies. I advised him to swap jobs, because Cunard provides many benefits to crew members. He did swap and was very grateful to me. We both had remarkable moments working on Queen Victoria. We managed to share a cabin and it was a pleasant time. We used to drink red wine, his passion, and tried beers that we bought in the different countries we visited. Of course, the habit was only for professional purposes, since we worked in the bars department! We had many good times in the crew bar, laughing at the jewels from what the passengers sometimes said.

A special place for us was Egypt and we visited three times. Once we went to see the pyramids, 200 kilometers away from Cairo, on a tour organized by the ship for crew members. I loved every moment and took hundreds of pictures. Visiting distant places such as Egypt has been my dream since childhood. But, after visiting the pyramids twice, we wanted to see something else. The trip to the pyramids takes ten hours, too much time to allow for sightseeing we already knew. Therefore, we decided to stay in Port Said, a poor town but a great opportunity to get to know a bit about the normal life of the Egyptians. We went out very early and chartered a taxi right at the port. The driver, Saed, a 60 year old man, explained to us that the country had no social security and therefore he was obliged to work to provide for his family. He was very sympathetic and charged us only ten dollars for the four-hour tour through the Egyptian suburbs. It may seem very little money to us, but for him it was good money. Saed was happy for the extra ten dollars we gave him as a gratuity.

The town was in chaos. There are no traffic lights and public transportation was a mess. Hygiene is something they cannot be proud of; butchers sell their products alfresco in the hot African midday. For Hector and me, it was interesting to see how an ancient country like that could still be underdeveloped and so miserable. We knew Brazilian slums, so there was nothing new to us, but the other crew members refused to visit the place. Hector and I have this in common—we love poor countries. Maybe because of the resemblance with my Boninal. Of course my hometown is not like Port Said, but it is far from being like a Norwegian city. By the way, Hector does not like Norway. He says the country works so well and that everything is so organized that he gets bored.

In spite of being poor, Port Said inhabitants received us very well. In order not to leave the place without a good story to tell, we searched for beers to improve our collection. As I said, for professional purposes only! However, in Egypt our pilgrimage for beer with any content of alcohol was a time-consuming and fruitless task. Because of religious beliefs Egyptians do not sell alcoholic beverages. When we finally found a place that supplied alcohol, the bartender talked to us as if we were doing something highly illegal. Anyway, we bought a six-pack that cost more than the taxi ride.

Next, we asked Saed to take us somewhere where we could eat a typical meal of his country. Definitely not a good idea as their food is completely different from mine. The menus are impossible to understand. Saed tried to help as much as he could but his lack of English was an obstacle. At last, we ordered a pizza of camel meat. But before that, unbelievably, we ate raw camel meat! I can prove it—I recorded a video showing us tasting this delicacy. We could not let Saed down, since he had been so nice to us. There we were in the street with two boxes improvised as a table and sharing the pizza that we swallowed with the help of large sips of Coke. We gave Saed the leftovers and he was happy to have something to take home for his family. I, my friend Hector and our stomachs will never forget that day.

Hector and Egypt

vimeo.com/115609944

Young and handsome but still my friend!

Another friend to whom I became closer to in that period was Fernando. By the time I finish this book, he will be on Queen Mary 2, the same ship in which I embarked on July 13th, 2013.

Fernando was born in the São Paulo state hinterland. He has worked on ships for three years and we met on Queen Victoria. He wears his hair short, smiles very easily and is always in a good mood. Because of his grandparents, he was able to gain Italian citizenship. He also lived in England before applying for a job in Cunard. He belongs to the restaurant department, therefore he works a lot more than Hector and I do. Even so he found time to be my biggest companion for adventures both on and off Queen Victoria. We played soccer in many countries. We rode bicycles in Spain in Barcelona and Cadiz as well as in Norway around Bergan and Kristiansand and some other places.

Just like me, he enjoys tasting different brands of beer. I recorded in video some of our tastings in Saint Thomas and Prince, Hawaii, Mexico, Guatemala, Costa Rica, Nicaragua, United States and other places.

We had a terrific day in Los Angeles. I booked us a chauffeured limousine. We were a group of ten crew members and we all wanted to visit the Hollywood sign. A limo is cheaper than a taxi in Los Angeles; there are many in the city and that is the reason why the cost is so low. For a five-hour tour, which included beverages, we agreed to pay US$450. This meant just US$45 for each one of us. Everything went OK, except for one thing. Sometimes before anyone can get off the ship, the local police make a surprise raid to check for drugs or smuggling. The officers bring trained dogs to sniff around the ship's crew. In situations like that we cannot leave the ship until the inspection is completed. That was what happened that morning. We did not worry though because we had plenty of time to meet the Limo at 10:00am. The problem was that a crew member from the Mauritius Islands was calmly doing something forbidden in most corners of the world including in the United States where it is not only forbidden, but criminal. He was smoking a cigarette of marijuana with the cabin door wide open for all to see. To make a long history short, his colleagues told us later that the crew member was very ashamed, and he had been kept in jail for two days in the United States before being deported back to his own country. Moreover, his passport was marked with red ink and he lost his license to work on ships.

Because of that mess, no crew members could leave the ship before 11:30am and we lost two hours of our city tour. Anyway, we still managed to have a good time in Los Angeles. We saw the Hollywood Sign from inside a chic limo equipped with vodka, whiskey, rap music and a beautiful female driver. We also visited Beverly Hills, the Hall of Fame and other tourist attractions. Since I already knew the city, the novelty for me was the limo.

One week before my ten-day vacation in London, Fernando and I stopped once more in Uncle Sam's land. It was a wonderful day in New York, because again I had won a competition for being the best drink sales person on-board. Fernando found someone to do his side job on port day and we enjoyed a full day in the Big Apple.

Young and handsome

vimeo.com/115609943

Black is beautiful

A third person who became my close friend was born in the Mauritius Islands, a small country that not many people have heard about. Allan is a tall and strong man. We met on the Queen Victoria. At that time he was getting his fourth professional promotion in less than three years and this time to the bars department. We both are outgoing and make friends easily so we got along very well. He is a cheerful man, in spite of having a troubled history like me. He had lost his mother, and his father had left him when he was a baby, so his grandmother raised him. He had fought quite a battle to get where he was. Nowadays he is the owner of a virtual communication enterprise on the Island of Mauritius. He is building the house of his dreams for his beautiful wife and his lovely daughter. Allan was responsible for my arrival onto the ship where I currently work. I will tell the whole history later. Now I want to write about the records.

Records

I bought in Miami, the most effective and economical piece of equipment to record everything that I want to document from my wanderings throughout the world. I love photos and videos. I have produced more than 3,000 videos since 2009, when I first sailed the seas. Before that I had already bought a digital camera and a laptop to edit my photos and videos. That was regular equipment let us say, just normal, compared to the one I dreamed of buying when I started working at Cunard. It may seem silly to some people, but I consider that acquisition a great achievement in my personal life. On December 6th, 2011, I was in Miami and decided to give myself an early Christmas present, which I had already been flirting with on the Internet. I told my manager that I had an urgent deal to make onshore and got leave for a four hour break. It was very early and I was the first crew member to get off the ship. I was anxious to buy the Apple MacBook Pro, a laptop computer that allows me to edit videos perfectly. It was not cheap, but I can say that it was worth every cent. I am very happy with it and whenever I decide to buy a new one, it is going to be an Apple computer.

On my new computer, I edited a video that has received—and still receives—thousands of views on YouTube. It is posted under the title *Imagine 56 nationalities Cunard*. The video consists of a single phrase in English and afterwards in the native language of the person who speaks it. One representative from all 56 nations that composed the then crew of Queen Victoria just states his/her name and their country of origin. My idea was to gather all crew members of Queen Victoria in one video, because many friends kept asking me about the nationalities of the people with whom I work. Talking to crew members of other countries, I realized that this curiosity is not only Brazilian. Tired of hearing that question and of losing time explaining over and over again the same stuff, I decided to make the video.

I started the interviews on January 22nd, 2012. The word about the initiative spread like a fever in the ship. I spent two months, going to each department of the ship, asking each crew member to state his/her name and country of origin, in English and in his/her mother language. In this way, even people who do not speak English could enjoy at least the part spoken in their own language and at the same time see where and how we work. In the beginning people were reluctant, shy or nervous of being in front of a camera; many of them did not even want to be recorded. Somehow, I finally recorded images of people of all nationalities aboard the Queen Victoria. It could have been 57, but a waitress from Estonia did not want to participate.

The video was an instant success. Four hours after I posted it, still in Aruba, my manager called me to his office to ask me for a copy of the video on a pen drive. He explained that the company monitors everything about it that goes to the Internet, and so wanted a copy. Cunard posted the video on its website, giving the credit to me. The entertainment manager even invited me to participate in one edition of the monthly crew talent show she organizes on the ship at the Royal Court Theater. She heard about the video and wanted to show the full version of my video. After the presentation, I had to address a few words to the audience. I spoke in English to more than 800 people. When I stepped onto the stage, with all those lights shining on my face, I trembled as never before. Hundreds of people applauding me, pleased with what they just saw in the video. Perhaps they were smiling, because at the end of the video I appear, dressed as a senior officer and presenting myself as the captain—of the video, of course…

The next day, I felt like a Hollywood star. Passengers played with me, calling me Queen Victoria's Captain. Still today, I receive emails from all over the world, congratulating me for the video "Imagine 56 Nationalities Cunard". I had to remake the video twice, to include a female friend from Slovakia

and to include the captain of the ship, who insisted on representing England. I am proud to say that this video is used today for a British shipping agency to sell maritime cruises.

56 Nationalities

goo.gl/12NvWN

C hapter 19

Both worker and tourist

One has to have good sense, traveling throughout the world. Working ten, twelve hours per day, with no Sundays off and no holidays. We, crew members, are hired to do that, I know, but someday I will be a passenger, and it will be my last promotion. This is something still to be achieved and I very much value this as a future goal.

Third dry dock

The third downtime for maintenance of which I participated, happened because of an emergency. The ship had a mechanical problem. Do not ask me what it was, because I have absolutely no idea; I am just repeating what the company informed us. I remember the moment when the captain, the first female captain in Cunard's ships, made an announcement through the loudspeaker system. Some passengers worried about the news. We, the crew, knew that it is a normal procedure and calmed down the guests.

Next thing I did was plan what to do with my time off when the ship was in dry dock. Marco Túlio Avellar, my cabin mate at that time and a novice in maritime life, when I invited him, thought that we would be doing something wrong by leaving the ship. He finally understood that we had permission to get off.

We discussed very well the itinerary, because we did not have much money. We selected three places to visit during our breaks, from October 3rd to 16th, and all of them distant from the sea. We were sick of seeing saltwater, after such a long time aboard, therefore, we took a wise decision: Munich, Prague and Vienna.

We traveled from Southampton to Munich by bus. The alternatives, airplane or train, were tremendously expensive. The most impressive thing on this trip was, definitely, the English Channel crossing. In Brazil we have some outstanding examples of architecture and engineering, like the 72 meters high Rio-Niterói Bridge, with its 13,290 meters over the Atlantic Ocean. However, it is impossible not to be amazed by the 35 kilometers (22 miles) tunnel under the water of the English Channel, linking England and France. It is quite impressive to see the amount of buses and cars taken underneath the Channel by trains. We reached Munich 24 hours later, exactly in the middle of the world famous Oktoberfest. The city is extremely well organized, as we could see at the bus depot. From there we took a train to the campsite, with capacity for 5,000 guests. Marco Túlio and I paid US$65 per day, each, to use a tent for two. It was a nice clean place. The only problem was my friend snoring all night!

We joined the Germans in the Oktoberfest, equivalent to a Brazilian Carnival. For US$8 a day, we could drink as much beer as we wanted in the campsite. I was pleased to know that Germans are not cold and indifferent people. On the contrary, they ate, drank and sang during the whole event. Each culture has its way to express joy and we should respect this. Do not think that I went to Munich only for the beer. I am interested in the culture of the countries. In Munich, we visited the Oktoberfest Museum, the BMW headquarters, the stadium where the first match of the World Soccer Cup of 2006 took place, the Allianz Arena, the National Stadium that hosted the Olympic games of 1972, the National Theater, the City Hall and the cathedral next to it. The experiences I had during those four great days made me curious about the Brazilian Oktoberfest, organized every year by the German citizens living in of the southern city of Blumenau.

Prague was included in our itinerary because of the family background of Marco Túlio. His grandfather lived there, back in the sixties, as the Brazilian ambassador. I did not have any information about the city. When we got there, I could understand why Marco Túlio wanted so much to visit that most individual place. We stayed in Prague for five days. It is not a huge city and we were able to go everywhere by foot. I took about 500 pictures there. The architecture is magnificent, mixing ancient and modern buildings. The main tourist attractions are located in the city center, the Old Town Square. There is an hourly mechanical show at the Orloj Astronomical Clock; for three minutes, puppets representing the 12 apostles come out of the window in the upper part of the time piece, with Saint Peter leading the parade. When the puppets go back inside the windows, the chimes of the hour can be heard. It is a fascinating event to watch; the crowds gather below it on the hour. Most Czechs speak English as a second language; they are well educated and warm. Czech gastronomy is remarkable. The beer is cheap and very good.

Vienna was our next stop, just 249 kilometers away from Prague. It is considered one of the best cities in the world to live. We also traveled by bus because it was the least expensive. We found a hostel to stay in, cheaper than the Munich campsite and much more comfortable. Vienna's architecture is similar to that we saw in Prague. The city, though, is cleaner and evidently wealthier. The Austrian transportation system is, for me, something cinematic. The word organization must be the first that children learn in Austria. People speak very good English. What impressed me most was my awareness of how good the security was there; nobody is likely to have their watch or laptop stolen on a bus, although we saw no police officers in the streets. Important personalities of the world history were born in Vienna, Freud for instance. Beethoven was born in Bonn, Germany, but lived in Vienna as a 22 year old. Mozart was born in Salzburg but he also lived in Vienna.

Schönbrunn Palace

bit.ly/1x2VfUv

On the last day of our stay in Austria, I decided to visit the hometown of a crew colleague, Monika Martonakova. She highly praises Bratislava, the capital of Slovakia, the other part of the former Czechoslovakia. It is near Vienna, just 60 kilometers away. Since I always talk about Boninal, it would be thoughtful to visit her city of birth. It is a nice city, but I have to confess that, after seeing Prague and Vienna, any other city of the world would not have the same enchantment.

To get back to Vienna we took a flight to London and from there a train to Southampton. Guess who we met on the train? Monika Martonakova. Coincidences. I do not need to tell you how happy she was to see the pictures of Bratislava. We had lunch together in Southampton and returned to the ship to go on with our work.

vimeo.com/116038715

Chapter 20

Back to the future

However back on-board, I wanted to take a longer break. I felt I needed some time to take care of my hotel and to recover from my broken relationship. I asked Cunard for six months leave and they agreed. But I guess the most important project for me was to write this book. I had so much wanted to write about my life so far. I also had a sense that this book may pave the way to my future and other dreams that I have.

Working on my book

By the time I disembarked at the Salvador Airport, coming from London, on November 23rd 2012, an idea was boiling in my brain. That decision was to write this book. Two friends, Emerson Fernando and Erone Feitosa, had already encouraged me to write. They said that I had many things to tell and that I should share with people what I have learned on my travels. They said I could show others an example of a regular man who worked with discipline and did not give up on his dreams.

That same November, in Boninal, I visited Emerson Fernando, currently the director of the same high school where I studied until my second year. He told me that he would help me to write the book and indeed we started the project a few days later. He prepared a summary of my aims and objectives for this very book. Then I passed the result to a journalist who helped me to transform these memories into a well-organized report, giving his touch to my writing to make the narrative accessible. The same journalist translated my original book into English. So from these beginnings, the world can now read about the boy who fought to achieve his conquests.

During that vacation period at Boninal—in fact a half vacation—I worked very much on this book and I kept recalling the ship, mainly because of the 800 people I added to my Facebook page during this time.

A break from writing

A common friend, Fernanda Cunha, whom I met on-board Queen Victoria, called me from Rio de Janeiro to tell me that she had a Danish friend and asked me to look after him for two weeks. I knew Fernanda quite well, since we rode bicycles in the Norway Mountains, so of course I said yes. She was happy and I was happy too.

So Asker came to stay in my mother's house. It was the second foreigner I took to my hometown—the first being the beautiful Alice. Asker is typically Danish, with green eyes and so blond that his hair seemed white. He is young but experienced, vegetarian, hot tempered and an extraordinary human being. He spent two weeks with me touring Brazil's northeast. The unusual thing about that visit was that I did not know him before this trip. Asker has a black soul in a white body. He loves the samba, reggae, carnival and Brazilian women. He took part in a capoeira demonstration, a Brazilian martial art, and was the center of attention because he was very good. We became great friends. I planned to visit him in Denmark as soon as I finished my six months contract on Queen Victoria. We said goodbye at Salvador Airport. He was going to meet someone in southern Bahia. I was going, once more, to São Paulo. This time to continue the work of running my hotel that I bought with my cousin Nadival, Uncle Didi's son, in São Caetano do Sul. I then lived in São Caetano do Sul for six months, working at the hotel, before I returned once again to sail the seven seas.

From my hotel, I kept in touch with the world, especially with crew members. I often talked to my friend Allan, who was on-board the Queen Mary 2. He kept saying that I had to embark again, to begin a new chapter of my life.

I completed my book, writing in my own language of Portuguese. I published this book myself and then launched it in several places throughout Brazil. The results were very interesting for a beginner writer like myself. Reviewing the text of this book in English, I realized that I could have written more about every country and every city I visited throughout the world, but it would have taken hundreds of pages more to record all my feelings and experiences.

Queen Mary 2

A ship is my floating home and I belong to the sea. I have no anchors restraining me. That is why I embarked again, on July 13th 2013. During any spare time that I had on-board, I gave the final touches to this book. As I write, I am, at this very moment on Queen Mary 2. She is the most famous ocean liner in the world and she is currently taking us back and forth across the Atlantic Ocean between Southampton and New York, a seven-day voyage. Given that she is a giant ship, I know that the work on board is hard, but I am prepared for work. For the sea however, I know that it is not possible to be completely prepared: the water is forever changing, the winds are forever changing and neither can ever be absolutely known.

Once more number thirteen brought me luck. On August 13th 2013, I completed the first month on board after my arrival at Heathrow Airport, in London, and it will probably be the last entry date of these humble memories before publishing them in English. I am in my cabin, 533 on my way to New York, where we will dock on the 15th. I may say that I am a lucky man. God Almighty was very generous to me.

Let me tell you the circumstances of my going back to sea.

I left Boninal, after my book launch, to go straight to London. Well, not a direct trip. From my hometown to London, I first needed to take a bus to the capital, Salvador, a ten-hour journey. I always travel one day in advance in order not to miss my flight. This year I took special care, because there were some strikes and demonstrations against the 2014 World Soccer Cup that is to be held in Brazil. The flight between Salvador and Lisbon took nine hours. The connecting flight between Lisbon and London took another three hours.

In summary, I left my mother's house on July 9th, by 10:00pm, and got to London on July 12th, by 10:30am, tired and feeling the full effects of jet lag. It was too early for checking in, so I had to wait until 2:00pm to get some rest.

Cunard is like a big family to me. No matter which of their ships I embark on, I always find someone I know. On my first night in London I shared a hotel room with Rinaldo, a Brazilian guy. To my surprise, among the 100 crew members at the hotel I met Marcos, a friend from Mauritius I knew from Queen Victoria. He speaks a little Portuguese and is very sociable. It was nice to meet a friendly face and it gave me confidence. As we had some hours before the hotel team prepared the room, I invited Marcos to go to the center of London, only 15 miles away from the airport. Different from how it is in Brazil, a train links the airport to the city center in a few minutes. And once again there I was, just as in 2010 when I first embarked for Cunard. London seemed to be having a party to receive me. The weather was hot, as I had never experienced before. Marcos and I visited Big Ben and the London Eye. It was heartwarming to be in England again, retracing my steps. It was a short walk. We went back to the hotel for a drink and dinner, welcoming crew members that arrived from many parts of the world.

The London Eye

bit.ly/1zeSdlM

The next day, July 13th, early in the morning, three buses waited for us. Everything happened as planned. I was both a little anxious as well as excited because I was going to meet some old friends and at least 1,200 other crew members that I had never seen before. We arrived at the Southampton port at 9:00am. The gigantic black vessel, the Queen Mary 2, was docked. A large quantity of equipment and thousands of people walked around the port. In less than three hours the ship would have 2,600 guests embarked and would start a seven-day voyage to Norway. Even on my fifth contract, I still felt butterflies in my stomach. When I got on the ship we went through the administrative procedures, handing passports, medical exam records and visas. We received instructions and uniforms with the help of the bar supervisor, who thankfully made everything easier. I attended the first training session before starting my shift. By 4:00pm I was at the Terrace Bar, ready for my first day of work. The departure was scheduled for 4:30pm. The size of Queen Mary 2 scared me. She is just huge, and yet at the same time beautiful and imposing. I am lucky to be here.

I met my friend Allan, a former colleague on the Queen Victoria. I am very proud of him. He is very talented. He started working as a buffet steward, then got a promotion to bar waiter and now is a bartender.

You might be asking, why did I not ever have a promotion? After three years, it would be natural. In fact, the Queen Victoria bar manager twice offered me the position of bartender, but I like being a bar waiter. Why? Because I am a very energetic person and I do not like to stay behind a bar. I need a roomy place to work in and I like to choose a person to talk to, exchanging ideas and experiences. At the Renaissance Hotel I almost assumed the position of security guard based only on the money—I would have regretted my choice forever. I am who I am because of the choices I made in the past.

It does not please me to sit behind a desk to do paper work. I do not dream about being a manager, although I admire those who do. The promotion I want is from crew member to passenger. I have come a long way and do not want to be better than anyone else. I just want to be happy doing what I do, being a bar waiter on a Cunard ship. Being here is very much a conquest for me. I need no more than that for the time being.

Of course, I want the comfort that money brings. But I need my spiritual comfort as well. In my hotel, in São Caetano do Sul, I am the general manager; this does not make me better than any person that works for me. We just work together to achieve a common objective for our business.

Here, in Queen Mary 2, I think it works in the same way. We need people in the front-line, with responsibilities. My duty is to be responsible for offering the passengers a service of excellence.

Routine: the good, the not so good and the unusual

My first month passed quickly, working as I was in three different bars. That is the routine and on every second trip we work in a different bar. The positive aspect to this routine is exactly that we do not have a routine. We are less distressed because the work is always different. I love to be a bar waiter because I work all over the ship, serving in different locations and consequently see and meet more people. As I love talking it makes my life better and happier. But there is a negative aspect too.

When I arrived in the Queen Mary 2, I started working with my Mauritian friend Sammy who was a bar supervisor, a nice person and a competent person too. He is an old acquaintance of mine. We first met on Queen Victoria and visited Norway together, played soccer and cooked barbecues around the world. On the Queen Mary 2, my first job was in the G32 Night Club. My shift ended at 3:00am or 4:00am. Three weeks later, I was assigned to the Sir Samuel Café Bar, which opened at 6:30am. Two weeks on and I was in the Commodore Club, where it is hard to say when the shift will end. I was aware of the situation when I signed the contract and my purpose here is to work, wherever they needed me. What I am saying is not a complaint but just an observation and the only small downside I found to working shift.

This leads me to another factor, which is very interesting, that I want to tell you about. Now imagine all our schedules constantly changing as the ship moves East. This happens because there are five one-hour shifts on the return journey but, each one is in a different time zone. In fact, on this route we travel through five time zones! The reverse situation occurs when we travel West. Here we have five one-hour shifts with the time zone moving forwards! On top of this, there is a particular curiosity for me: during a crossing we do not have *noon* for five days in a row and so, on these days, the clocks change straight from 11:59am to 1:00pm.

Even with these challenges, we manage to build a happy environment—not only for the guests but also for the crew members.

Me as President Obama!

When I worked at the Renaissance Hotel, Lucas, the door attendant, gave me the nickname of Obama. I did not take the joke seriously at that time, but, when I started working on my first ship, one year later, one of the first things I heard from American passengers was that I resembled President Barak Obama. On the Queen Victoria, in 2010, everybody knew me as *El Presidente*. So because I was Obama, this meant that Alice was known as the First Lady. It was when I was on the Queen Mary 2 that I came to realize that I might actually look like the United States' President Obama. On one occasion, this was the very first thing a colleague said to me, and he did not know me at all at that stage!

She who is the Queen of the seas

Queen Mary 2, like any Cunard ship, is a dream for anybody who wants to work on ships. She is the greatest and the fastest ocean liner in the world. There are two special things about her. Everything on board is big and she has a commander who is the Commodore of the entire fleet. As a crew member, it is a privilege for me to be one of the 1,250 workers on board. For example, by the time this book was finished, I had visited New York, one of the best cities in the world, six times and I got off the ship there five times. Queen Mary 2 was definitely my promotion in the company. My aim is that my next promotion will be to that of a passenger as I sell my book around the world!

I am working aboard again because, having accomplished the dream of buying a hotel, I want to take advantage of my experience to achieve other dreams. I want to be a part of the Queen Mary 2 history and I also want to buy an apartment to have my own safe port, my own "dry dock". In there, I will display all the souvenirs that I've bought in each port, including my collection of 50 shot glasses with the names of the countries I visited. On the walls, I will hang my favorite pictures. In fact, I would like to put them all up, since in a way they all are momentous. But, what the heck, there are 40,000 of them… I would need a warehouse!

My apartment will be an extension of my mind. With one enormous difference—what is kept inside my mind will never be burnt, robbed or erased. My memories of the sea are the essence of who I am!

Everything I have been through and experienced on Queen Mary 2 was genuine and is authentic. This confirms and proves to me that all I've done, and where I am now taking my life, is both just and reasonable. I know that my history with this fantastic ship has not ended yet. I want to sail with her again. I want to learn and understand more about a ship that causes so much curiosity. Who knows? Maybe I will write a book about the Queen Mary 2. Or maybe I will write about some other of my yet untold tales of life and adventure.

To you, my reader, who accompanied me up to these final pages, my warmest regards.

For me, it has all been worth it.

Thank you!

Final thoughts

FINAL COMMENTS FROM A DEAR FRIEND

I am very happy this autobiography of my friend Martinês is delivered to the world in this way. He is putting into practice the old Brazilian phrase that goes something like this: every man should have a child, plant a tree and write a book.

I have my doubts about him not having an heir, somewhere in the world.

As for planting a tree, my friend is a nature lover and he certainly has planted many.

The third part of the sacred trilogy comes now, with this book. Martinês' Story is also a part of my history, because I lived with him, a joyous experience of being a poor boy on Down Street in our small village of Boninal.

I truly believe that we are both winners. Failure was not written in our fate. We have taken part in writing this script; a script that proudly tells so much about us and our lives.

When my little boy Samuel asks me how my childhood was, I will not hesitate in taking this book from the shelf and using it as a compass for my memory.

I will then show it to him letting him know that this book contains a guide for living a worthwhile life.

I will also tell him of the importance of knowledge and education and where it can take us.

Emerson Fernando

Printed in Australia
AUOC02n0035080217
282797AU00004BA/4/P

9 781925 198003